HOUSEKEEPING

HOUSEKEEPING

for HOTELS

MOTELS

HOSPITALS

CLUBS

SCHOOLS

GRACE H. BRIGHAM

Former Hotel Housekeeping Consultant, American Hotel Association
Past President, National Executive Housekeepers' Association

REVISED EDITION

Ahrens Series

HAYDEN BOOK COMPANY, INC.
Rochelle Park, New Jersey

Housekeeping

for Hotels, Motels, Hospitals

Clubs, Schools

81703

Copyright, 1955, 1962, by the

AHRENS PUBLISHING COMPANY, Inc.

Library of Congress Catalogue Card Number: 62-20848

First Edition 1955

Revised Edition, 1962

9   PRINTING

73 74 75 76 77 78   YEAR

Manufactured in U. S. A.

To
the National Executive Housekeepers' Association which,
since 1930, has been working toward a professional standing
for the Executive Housekeepers in American institutions,
and to
the young people who are training for hotel careers, I
sincerely hope this reference book may be of value.

GRACE H. BRIGHAM

Foreword

Housekeeping is one of the most significant contributions to the library of management. It is a work of major importance.

The Author has made a great and lasting contribution in advancing the professional status of Housekeeping Management, an aim to which she has completely dedicated her life and work.

One of the most modest executives I have ever been privileged to know, Mrs. Grace H. Brigham, is a person of unequalled experience, not only as an Executive Housekeeper in major hotels in the United States, but in her depth of knowledges and areas of professional contribution which go much further. She has been a teacher and department head, consultant, decorator, engaged in corporate research, prolific writer, author and lecturer, college and university faculty member. In addition she has an amazing record of active leadership responsibilities in professional, civic, national and international organizations too numerous to mention.

A Charter Member of the National Executive Housekeepers' Association and Honorary Life Member, Mrs. Brigham's treatment of a difficult subject area, for management and particularly housekeeping management as an art as well as a science, has overlooked nothing in this remarkable work. It brings to every reader a clear and direct understanding of the size, scope and complexity of Housekeeping Management. And it covers the techniques, multiple skills, knowledges and responsibilities of the Executive Housekeeper or Housekeeping Manager, who is the principal operating executive concerned with maintaining and protecting the major source of revenue and profit in hotels, motels, clubs, hospitals and institutions today.

This book will be valued and appreciated by the professional as well as the student, and it is also for those in top management who really want to know about, and are concerned with effective House-keeping Management. As one of many who were privileged to read this manuscript, it was clear to me that it contains more information about the organization and management of this vital function than has ever before been written on the subject.

HERBERT K. WITZKY
Head, Hotel & Restaurant
Management Program
New York University

Contents

Part I. THE HOUSEKEEPER'S DUTIES

Part II. EMPLOYEES

CONTENTS

Introduction

Most institutions (hotels, motels, hospitals, clubs; school dormitories, etc.) employing an Executive Housekeeper, are engaged in selling specialized services to the public. These institutions may vary in size and type. They may be located in large or small cities, in towns, in the country, on the desert, at the seashore, or in the mountains, but *all* depend for success on satisfying their guests. Their basic problems are similar though their services may differ as widely as those of a Y.M. or Y.W.C.A., a college or university, a bank, a church, or a steamship line.

Clubs are formed for the use of a group of congenial people interested in recreation of various kinds. Usually they furnish food, often beverages, a limited number of sleeping and reception rooms for guests, perhaps a library. A large part of the building, however, is devoted to a gymnasium, swimming pool, Turkish bath, various kinds of game rooms, etc. Country clubs also provide a golf course, tennis court, and other outdoor recreational facilities.

The function of hospitals is to aid sick people in regaining their health. They have reception rooms for visitors, recreation and rest rooms, often sun rooms or open porches for patients, dining rooms for the staff, doctors' and nurses' living quarters which are usually located in separate buildings similar to small hotels. Executive offices, diet and regular kitchens, and housekeeping quarters are also necessary. However, the greatest amount of floor space is given over to bedrooms for one, two, three, or four patients, and wards for many patients.

Most of the space in hotels and motels is devoted to sleeping rooms. Function and dining rooms are usual and frequently entertainment is furnished. Today's hotels and motels are so similar that usually they are comparable in many ways. Both cater to salesmen, tourists, vacationers, and travelers of many kinds and a few have permanent guests. Convention facilities are becoming increasingly popular in motels.

Sales in all of these institutions depend on pleasing the public.

If the public is to be pleased, all such institutions must keep all public, function, and sleeping rooms in first class condition with the largest possible number ready for sale as needed. Good or bad housekeeping management may be largely responsible for high or low occupancy. This is one of the important production departments offering rooms "packaged" for sale. If the package does not suit the buyer, there will be unoccupied rooms and this department's daily sales revenue (40 to 60 percent of income) is not met. Unfortunately this cannot be made up the next day. Any day's unsold rooms are a total loss.

If patrons are pleased with the condition of rooms and the quality of service, they will return often and take pleasure in telling friends of the fine accommodations and service. There is no more valuable advertising than this. Anything less than complete satisfaction has just the opposite effect and is very difficult to combat.

There are few managers or administrators who do not employ an executive housekeeper, accountable to them for the appearance of the entire house. Experience has proved that such a person, when given full responsibility and authority, saves top management many headaches. We will henceforth refer to the housekeeper as of the feminine gender because women are still filling the majority of these positions. When a man is thus employed he is often given a different title.

Since no two women use exactly the same methods in keeping their houses clean, and in order, no two executive housekeepers manage their departments in precisely the same way. Even in large chain operations where procedures are carefully outlined and coordinated, allowances are made for differences in size, location, type of house, labor conditions, and other circumstances. We can cover here only basic functions and a few variations in method.

Whether there are 50, 500, or 2500 rooms, management wants this department run with the highest degree of efficiency in order to please the guest and at the lowest cost possible.

The foregoing is a very abbreviated description of an extremely

complex undertaking since it also involves the housekeeper's relations with and obligations to her immediate superior, other department heads, her own staff, and other employees. This is not an easy
task and the difficulties increase with the size of the house. Success
is dependent largely on wisely chosen, well oriented, thoroughly
trained, and efficiently supervised employees whose high morale
means willing and close cooperation.

About 75 percent of the members of the American Hotel Association and the large majority of motels have 75 rooms or less, so it
seems appropriate to begin our study of housekeeping with the
various types of operation and the problems of these smaller houses.

GRACE H. BRIGHAM

Part I

THE HOUSEKEEPER'S DUTIES

CHAPTER 1

The Small Hotel or Motel

Here, in a house of 75 rooms or less, the housekeeper is in direct charge of the linen room. In a larger house it is necessary for her to have an assistant to relieve her of certain duties such as—much of the care of the linen room, some inspection of guest and other public rooms and offices, the keeping of some records, often some mending and make-over. This person's duties will vary with the size of the house. When the housekeeper is alone there should be a head maid trained for relieving her in the linen room when her duties take her elsewhere. It is important that this person be recognized by other workers as the one best suited for this responsibility or she will have a difficult time at first. In some houses they vote by secret ballot for the one they think best to fill this position. In one house the vote was so close that two maids were used alternately. It worked out well.

When she has no assistant, the housekeeper opens the linen room before the employees arrive. She assigns the workers to their stations giving them any necessary instructions. She distributes to them guest supplies, cleaning cloths, dusters, glass towels, and keys. They must sign for the latter. If they are in uniform, she inspects their appearance. When lockers are located at their stations, she does this inspecting on her first trip through the house.

Distribution of Linen

Most small houses either rent their linen or have it laundered outside for reasons of economy. When it is returned from the laundry it is delivered directly to the linen room for distribution. Usually in hotels, a houseman makes an afternoon delivery to the maids' closets on the floors to take care of early morning needs. If not, the maids carry a definite number of pillow slips, face and bath towels up with them in the morning and a houseman distributes the heavier pieces

3

at the same time. Motels that have rooms and apartments on the ground floor only, usually have the maid's cart fully packed and ready for her to wheel out to her station.

Breakfast linen is usually distributed the night before in order that the linen for lunch and for any afternoon or evening functions may wait until the morning rush is over. Dinner linen is usually distributed at the same time or in the afternoon.

Vacancy Lists

The time for making up a list of vacancies varies somewhat with the type of institution. Usually it is the first duty of each maid to check the actual condition of the rooms in her station—occupied, vacant, out-of-order, light baggage, or "sleep-out," and note the information on her vacancy list. Only when guests are out of the room can she indicate the amount of baggage or number of occupants so she must advise the linen room of these conditions later. These vacancy slips may be collected by the houseman on his linen delivery trip, by a bellman, or, if there is a service elevator, they may be hung on a hook beside it and taken to the linen room by the operator. The housekeeper transfers this information as it is received from the various maids to one list for the room clerk, notifying him of baggage and single or double occupancy as soon as she receives it.

Inspection

As soon as possible the head maid is called to take over the linen room while the housekeeper goes on inspection. If there is no head maid she locks the room and notifies the telephone operator where she will go first—usually to see that public spaces are in good condition. From there she goes to the top of the house or, in a motel of one story, to the unit farthest away, notifying the operator when she goes elsewhere.

She begins with check-outs and notifies the room clerk of each room that is ready for re-sale. One or two occupied rooms in each section are spot-checked as time permits, making a list of the rooms where something needs attention. She tries to spot-check every room at least once a week.

Unless it is a case of emergency, she waits to notify the various shops or departments of needed repairs until her return to the linen room. This saves her own, the telephone operator's, and the shop's time by not reporting each thing separately.

She returns to the linen room before lunch time to receive from maids their reports, guest's requests, lost and found articles, and from the housemen the morning's soiled linen. Usually a large duck bag is kept in each linen closet on the floors to hold soiled linen. This bag is tagged with the section and floor. Usually a list of all the different pieces of linen used is given to the maid and on this she checks off each item of soiled linen as she takes it from her cart. At the end of each morning and afternoon, the housekeeper totals these slips, signs them, and puts each in its respective bag. This is then tied tightly with the tag attached marking the section from which it came, and left for the houseman to take to the linen room where a recount is made unless the laundry is charged by the pound.

When clean linen comes in, the count is compared with the housekeeping record and any shortages or overages must be reported back to the laundry at once. A record must be kept as a settlement of these differences is made before payment of the invoice. Laundries should send torn, burned, or stained pieces back in a separate bundle. This is a great help to the always busy housekeeper. The houseman is directed how to put the clean linen back on the linen room shelves if there is no one else to do it.

Lunch time should come for the housekeeper after the maids and housemen have gone back to work for the afternoon so that she may be relieved or lock up the linen room and eat peacefully in the dining room. She needs a short rest also if she is to carry on effectively through the afternoon.

Afternoon Duties

Dining rooms must be required to send for dinner and banquet linen at a stated time so as not to interfere with afternoon procedures. The afternoon inspection routine is similar to the morning one, but there are usually more rooms into which she can go as many more guests are out. If she finds out-of-order rooms she tries to get them ready for rental as soon as possible. At all times she inspects all workers, new and old, to encourage, praise, or direct changes in method. She calls on any sick guests to offer what help she can and if there are permanent guests, she calls on one or more each day.

Records to Be Kept

On returning to the linen room she works on the many records which are required: window washing, wall or carpet washing, painting, floor polishing, cleaning furniture and uncarpeted floors, vacuuming, and any contract work. She may also have requisitions to make for new linen, equipment, supplies of various kinds, new carpets or draperies, or furniture to be re-upholstered. She also makes out work requisitions for the next day so that painters, polishers, upholsterers, carpenters, or electricians from outside will not be delayed in starting their work. At stated intervals there are linen inventories to be taken and the results sent to the manager.

As time permits, there are torn and burned pieces of linen to be mended or made into smaller items if it seems worth while; if not they are discarded. It is imperative that *no discards* be made by anyone except the housekeeper who carefully records this work for inventory purposes.

Conference with Manager

There are weekly or possibly daily conferences with the manager. However, a good housekeeper prides herself in not bothering him with petty details but solves small problems herself. When a complaint is made, she finds out who or what is the cause by consulting the ones involved, apologizes to the guest, rectifies the fault where possible and gives the manager the full report. If it's something she cannot handle, she tells him about it at once, giving full details from her investigation. A compliment is also passed along, not only to him but to the employee whose work induced the praise. She shares pride with all workers at the department meetings and also tells them of her embarrassment over any justified criticism, emphasizing that the more efficient the department is, the fewer the complaints.

Late Afternoon and Evening Duties

On their way out, maids bring their lists of afternoon vacancies to the linen room for the room clerk's information. They also turn in soiled dusters, glass towels, aprons, and articles left by guests in room check-outs during the afternoon. They leave a list of cleaning and guest supplies needed for the next morning, tell of any unusual happenings or guests' actions and turn in keys which are signed for. The housekeeper makes out passes for any articles to be taken out of the building after inspecting it. She then seals the packages with a "pass" sticker in such a way that they cannot be opened without detection.

Housemen hand in their lists of spaces cleaned, rooms vacuumed, and special work done. If there is a cleaning woman, she reports cleaning of maids' toilets, locker rooms, sink closets, stairs, terrazzo and marble borders of corridors, etc. Without such a person, this work is divided between maids and housemen. In motels there are also men who care for the grounds but these are not always under the housekeeper's supervision.

Working Hours

Maids' and housemen's daily hours are usually 8 A.M. to 4 P.M. except for those who service offices and public rooms. The latter may be scheduled from 7 A.M. to 3 P.M. or 7:30 A.M. to 3:30 P.M. as seems best. On Sundays and holidays workers are customarily scheduled one half or one hour later to suit the guests' convenience. One maid may be assigned to come in at the regular time to take care of early morning calls. Those who care for offices do their extra cleaning on Sundays—vacuuming, mopping, and polishing tile or linoleum floors, washing mirrors and glass tops of tables and desks, cleaning light fixtures, polishing furniture, etc. An analysis of requirements sometimes shows that staggered working hours save payroll dollars.

Night Workers

The night maids' hours and those of night housemen are decided by local conditions. They may be noon to 8 P.M., 1 to 9 P.M., 2 to 10 P.M., 3 to 11 P.M. or 4 to midnight. These maids service all women's lavatories for dining rooms and cocktail lounges nightly and, at stated intervals, the function rooms when they are used. Between times, she stays in the linen room where she may be reached as needed. While there, she gets the day maids' supplies ready as requested, wrapping them in a clean dust cloth and placing the list with the name on top of them. When clean aprons and uniforms are scheduled, she places this bundle on top also. If there is time she may do some mending between any necessary make-ups. She checks room occupancy when requested by the room clerk, makes sure all the linen closets are locked, and writes a report of any requests, instructions for morning, or unusual happenings for the housekeeper. She leaves this report and the keys with the room clerk.

This night maid must be chosen with care for this position requires a special kind of person. She must, of course, be an efficient maid. Also, she must be very adaptable for there will be many demands made on her and they must be met calmly and intelligently. She must be completely trustworthy and willing to carry out instructions. In fact, she must be a woman with latent abilities which will fit her for the position of assistant to the housekeeper for she represents the department head at night when the housekeeper is off duty. Such paragons are really in existence but if there are none on the staff, take the best there is and train her for the job. It will mean longer and irregular hours at first but it will be more than worth the effort.

The late houseman may work 10 P.M. to 6 A.M., 11 to 7 A.M. or 12 to 8 A.M. as conditions demand. He does the night cleaning in dining and cocktail lounges—also the bars—in the order in which they close. He cleans all the public lavatories and may be the one trained to take care of overnight check-outs when rooms may be sold if they are in order. His last duties are sweeping and hosing sidewalks.

It may be necessary to have an additional houseman on duty from 4 P.M. to midnight to assist the late houseman, especially if there are many evening functions. He should take tare of the men's lavatories for function, dining rooms, and cocktail lounges at stated times, clean back elevators, back stairways, and other service spaces, polish fire extinguishers, take care of sand jars, and many other things. If there is no extra man scheduled for these hours, it may be possible to stagger the hours of a day and midnight man to cover necessary work.

Suggestions

Following are a few ways to make work easier and build morale at the same time. Have on hand a file giving the various experiences and talents of every employee. Get this information from new employees when hiring them. If there are those who have been in your employ about whom you do not have this information, find it out. If they hesitate, tell them you want the information to use for their own betterment. If one is a good seamstress, she can help on a slow day with linen room mending, thus training her for regular relief and next in line for the position when it is vacant.

Another employee might like figures or have had some bookkeeping experience. Let her help with the linen inventory. Office and telephone skill could be useful also, if not in your department another department might be glad to borrow her in an emergency. There should be a relief worker trained for every sort of job, even in a small house. This is especially true of the night workers.

It is to be hoped that someone who is an excellent maid will prove, after thorough training, able to teach new comers. In a small house it is most difficult for the housekeeper to find time for intensive training because of many interruptions and demands on her time. If she must constantly stop and start her training work, it is confusing to a new employee and hard on the teacher also. If there is no alternative, talk over with the manager what duties can best be omitted during the training period. If his policy is "promotion from within" this training encourages the ambitious employee, reduces both training time and cost and is one factor in creating high morale. Another suggestion is the evidence of your interest in the workers' comfort and welfare by making sure their locker, rest and lunch rooms are clean, comfortable, and attractive. There are so many ways in which you can make them feel the importance of their part in the work of the hotel by praising them for good work and extra effort to please guests. "Do as you would have others do to you" is still an excellent motto.

Housekeeper's Hours

The housekeeper's work day is supposed to be from 7:30 A.M. to 4:30 P.M. but she often stays over to finish reports, plan changes in work routines, rearrange time schedules, and do many other things connected with her work. If she lives in the house she is on call at any hour for an emergency but if she has well trained night workers and if there is an efficient, considerate person in the front office, she is seldom disturbed. However, there must be a complete outline of night work procedures for the hours after the linen room closes and dependable people for carrying them out.

A standard emergency stock of guest room supplies and bedding must be left for making up a necessary check-out. Whoever uses these must leave soiled for clean or with a signed note giving the list of guest supplies used, the room number, and the time the room was made up. The closet where emergency supplies are kept must be checked every morning and replacements made when necessary. The key is kept at the room clerk's desk and he is responsible for giving it out. Any late check-outs that are not needed may be left for the day maid and the housekeeper notified.

There has been no mention made of the many emergencies that may come up during the day: guests' or employees' illness or accidents, losses or thefts, unexpected breakdown of essential equipment, leaks, floods, fires, storms, or tornadoes. Any of these may occur during a day and the housekeeper must not panic. Be assured, there is nothing monotonous about this job!

CHAPTER 2

The Housekeeper's Responsibility to Management

Labor and materials needed to keep an institution in first class condition are so costly today that good administration of the housekeeping department is imperative. The person in charge must be experienced, have a well-rounded education, the qualifications and the executive ability to meet and solve all sorts of problems and situations.

Perhaps it may be easier to grasp the skills necessary if some of the things top management expects of the executive housekeeper are listed:

1. Unless there is a personnel department, the housekeeper recruits, hires, trains and supervises (sometimes through others) the number and kinds of workers required. Each job must be analyzed and specifications made to discover the physical, mental, and personality qualities needed. From these, training procedures and work schedules are outlined.

2. She should have definite ideas on merit rating or other advancement policies unless these are already established.

3. In large or chain operations, she only specifies the kind of cleaning materials and equipment needed to take care of the various surfaces, guest supplies, and other material for which she is responsible. In smaller houses she does the buying as well as arrange for the storing and distribution of these items. Of course, she checks their receipt, keeps careful track of their use with a record of the length of time each lasts for a comparison with the claims made by salesmen.

4. She is accountable for the care of all sorts of floors and floor coverings, furniture, drapery and upholstery materials, glass curtains, Venetian blinds and accessories, plus bath and bed linens and bedding. It takes varied and specialized information to see that these are

all well chosen and cared for properly in order to get full value for their cost.

5. She requisitions, receives, stores, and distributes everything needed for setting up bedrooms and meeting rooms, extra furnishings for peak periods or special requirements for meetings or functions—the latter after consulting the sales manager and the head of the banquet department. In some houses, each of these department heads do their own buying or requisitioning and have their own storerooms. This is a fact the new housekeeper must learn before ordering.

6. The linen room is under her direction and its efficiency or lack of it, shows up quickly and has an important effect on the relations between the housekeeping department and the guests, other departments, and housekeeping employees.

7. There are many records for which the housekeeper is accountable:

   a. Time book, payroll, and automatic raises from merit rating or Union contract agreements.

   b. Schedules of days off, sick leave, vacations, and replacements.

   c. Records of contract work, its inspection, and approval of invoices for the work.

   d. Requisitions, records of all stock and equipment with card catalogue of reliable sources of supply.

   e. Receipt of all new supplies, equipment, furniture, carpets, materials, accessories, and uniforms, approval of invoices, date of issue for use, and length of service.

   f. Linen control: inventories, taking into account discards, losses, and replacements.

   g. Production of linen seamstresses, drapery and upholstery workers, and other maintenance workers on the payroll.

   h. Record of all work done, rooms washed, painted or papered, carpets laid or washed, placing of new furniture or polishing that which is already in the rooms, windows washed, etc.

   i. Inventory of furnishings in all rooms.

   j. Budgets and forecasts.

   k. Records of lost and found department—by whom found and date and to whom articles were returned, name, and date. In some houses this work is under the security officer.

   l. Employee accident reports and those for guests when these occur in an area of the building or its surroundings for which the housekeeping department is responsible.

   m. Guest cards to show requests made, preferences, dislikes or complaints regarding furnishings, service, or employees.

   n. A copy of any part of Federal, State, or local labor laws and Union contract affecting this department is necessary to avoid trouble.

8. Courteous and hearty co-operation with all other department heads is required as outlined later, in addition to excellent guest relations.

9. It may be that assistance in planning decorations is required. If a professional decorator has charge of this, the housekeeper must supervise the workmen to see that the decorator's orders are executed. When the work is completed, the housekeeper must be sure that furnishings are kept in the original places and that color schemes are adhered to when replacements must be made for cleaning, etc.

10. Effective communications are a most important part of the housekeeper's administrative responsibilities. As the coordinating link between management and employees, she must translate management's policies and directives to her staff in such a way as to help them realize that these are intended to keep both guests and employees happy by using money, equipment, and labor to the very best advantage. How well she succeeds has a direct effect on morale.

CHAPTER 3

The Executive Housekeeper's Responsibility to Guests

The American Hotel claims that "Guest Conditioning" is necessary for the success of any Institution. People really do "want what they want, when they want it" and will go where they come nearest to getting it. An Executive Housekeeper, therefore, plays a large part in keeping guests happy and encouraging their return—or the opposite.

The Importance of Training

Before beginning the training process, she must analyze every job in order to find those best suited for each kind of work—physically, mentally, and emotionally. Then there must be a definite work picture of what is to be done and how, followed by full explanation and intensive training in order to make the correct routine a habit. Even then, it must be followed by unceasing and strict supervision. This education for proper service must include attitudes, appearance, and freedom from offensive body odors, bad breath, and unpleasant habits, like gum chewing, whistling, or other loud noises—anything that might disturb the quiet, so much appreciated. Genuine courtesy is of paramount importance. Even if inborn this virtue has to be cultivated and the example of courteous consideration by all supervisory personnel in their relations with employees is an effective means of developing this quality and of increasing morale.

Everyone *must* be made to realize that the guests are the most important people in the place for they keep it in business and pay the wages. Explain that every establishment in the hospitality business aims to give each patron a sense of being welcome from the first contact at the front door to the last goodby. Help them to realize their important part in this. If they radiate friendly good will, the desire to please and thoughtful consideration for the guest's comfort,

14

it may encourage a longer stay, but definitely leaves the impression, "This is a good place to stay." Only the worker who enjoys the work can sell the guest in this way.

Striking roadside signs, colorful magazine advertisements, interesting radio and television presentations may persuade people to go to a place once, but their return depends on the opinion they form of the condition of rooms, quality of food, and general attitude of all employees. The poor impression made by even one careless, inefficient, slovenly or rude person can counteract the most expensive advertising and such an opinion is very hard to overcome.

Women Guests

Many women travelling alone are selling and have definite territories, so their repeat business is valuable. Others are in various professions, often speaking to local organizations. In both these cases their impressions of the hotel or motel will be given locally and across the country in either complimentary terms or the opposite. Their satisfaction with conditions is valuable, so in some houses the Housekeeper or her assistant is expected to call and see if there is any way in which they can be made more comfortable. The long mirror to see if one's slip shows, the high rod for long dresses are now standard equipment but sometimes extra hangers or blankets, etc., are welcomed.

Requests, Compliments, Complaints

Requests are greater than the other two combined and may be astounding at times, like the sailor boy who asked for a hammock because he had become accustomed to one in the Navy. A cot without a mattress (using two bedpads instead) met with approval and the guest called next morning to say he now knew what to ask for all the way across the country. The usual ones are attended to at once, if possible, and if the thing desired is not available that is explained. When asked for something not in stock, but often requested, the manager should be advised of the situation and asked about ordering it.

Complaints can be quite as surprising, as for instance the removal of an Audubon picture because "Birds in a room are bad luck." Justifiable complaints of a condition are immediately apologized for, investigated, the worker reprimanded and the supervisor questioned as to how it escaped her attention. When the complaint is about the action of an employee, both sides are heard before action is taken. By asking the worker "What happened in such a room?" the employee's point of view is discovered and usually found to be one of poor judgment, not intentional rudeness. A calm "Next time a thing like that happens, it would be better to — — —" is far better than a "bawling out."

Compliments are quickly and gladly passed on to the help for extra service rendered, or to management for approval of general praise.

The wise executive keeps the manager informed of all three of these, so that he may have a clear picture of guests' reaction and thus plan for satisfying them more fully. Be sure when telling him about the complaints to admit it if your department is at fault. Do not make excuses but explain the situation, tell him what you have done to prevent its recurrence or, if you do not know what to do, ask his advice.

When a guest is ill or in trouble of any kind, the housekeeper is naturally expected to be of the greatest help possible. For use in illness there must be ice and hot water bags, and various other hospital equipment ready for use when requested by Doctor or nurse. Medication of any kind is avoided because of the many allergies from which people suffer. The extra things in the storeroom may include allergy proof pillows, rubber and hair mattresses, bed boards, and means of lengthening a bed for the circus giant.

This department furnishes "baby sitters" and so many other helpers that each employee's skills must be known and used as needed. When the laundry is not able to wash a shirt on time or the valet is too busy to press a dress or an awkward dancer has torn a debutante's gown, there is always someone who can be spared to take care of the need. The list of what this Department is called on to do could be lengthened indefinitely, but the important thing is to realize the necessity for meeting guests' needs promptly and competently.

Guest Safety

Every effort must be made to guard the guest's safety, to guard against accidents in any part of the hotel or motel serviced by employees. This is successful only when the staff has been made so safety conscious that they are alert to any conditions that might cause accidents—the turned up rug corner, open carpet seam, splintered chair. leg or any other accident hazard caused by carelessness.

CHAPTER 4

The Housekeeper's Responsibility to Other Department Heads

The manager of the small hotel actually supervises all phases of the work and settles all questions as to *who* does *what* and *how* it should be done. With increased size, efficiency demands division of the work into departments, with the head of each directly responsible to him. These divisions differ according to conditions, but many are separated into six or seven divisions of the working staff.

1. *Rooms and Front Office*—supervised by an assistant manager— handles reservations, assigns rooms, and keeps necessary records. He is often in charge of the security officer, telephone service, and perhaps uniformed service, which includes doormen, bellmen, messengers, elevator operators, and porters.

2. *Food and Beverage*—responsibility often divided between maitre d'hotel, chef and steward—under the supervision of an assistant manager.

3. *Publicity and Sales*—responsible for bringing in new business, such as meetings, conventions, civic activities, and various functions—often directly responsible to the manager.

4. *Auditing*—accountable to the treasurer—takes care of all receipts, disbursements, leases, controls of glass, silver, linen, food and liquor.

5. *Engineering*—under the chief engineer—furnishes heat, light, power, and is in charge of maintenance.

6. *Housekeeping*—in charge of the Executive Housekeeper who is answerable for the conditions of all rooms and public spaces.

It is absolutely necessary for all of these inter-dependent divisions to cooperate fully for efficient and economical operation, for friction is like sand in machinery.

Except in large chains, there are many differences in management methods. New department heads must be told how they are expected to coordinate their work with the others. When this is not done it leads to friction, so it would seem advisable to begin work specifications at this level, for the highest efficiency.

Assistant Managers

The number of this type of employee varies, but there are at least three to cover the 24 hours. Housekeeping reports to the assistant manager include those of suspicious actions, out-of-the-ordinary occurrences, valuable finds, guest's complaints or requests that cannot be filled (and why). This should be done as quickly as possible and in full detail so he will understand the circumstances before the guest gets to him. He often goes with the housekeeper on inspection tours (if there is "white glove" testing) to find excellent maids for praise and usually prizes. In small difficulties or when the general manager is not available, the housekeeper turns to him for advice, so that the manager need not be disturbed except for major problems.

Room Clerk

Since it is recognized that the housekeeper is responsible for one of the principal commodities the hotel has for sale—rooms—both room clerk and sales manager expect her to provide the number and kind of rooms they want, when they are needed. However, she can do this only when given the information she needs at the time necessary. For instance, the speedy preparation of rooms for resale depends on *immediate* notification of their vacancy—no delay till there are several to be put on the telautograph. Likewise, the room clerk's work is simplified when checkouts are made up promptly and he is told at once. This prevents that first bad impression received when a guest is put in a room not yet in order. Except in emergencies, he is consulted before a room is put out of order to avoid confusion about a reservation.

It should be a rule to notify the housekeeper of guest changes to another room, so that articles left behind can be sent there instead of to the Lost and Found. If this is not done, there is apt to be confusion if the person sends for something missed when unpacking.

The number of the last room is given, whereas the old one is the one recorded. Unless there is a definite description, it may not be located and a bad impression is made. It is customary for the room clerk to do a certain amount of daily inspection as this gives him a familiarity with the rooms which enables him to meet individual needs more easily. After seeing a newly decorated suite, for instance, he is much less likely to assign it for a cocktail party than to see that Mr. and Mrs. VIP get it.

When there are numerous requests for the same room or section it would help the housekeeper if she could know why. Are the rooms especially attractive or quieter? Is it because of the view, the summer breeze, winter sunshine, or is the maid service extra good and if so, how? If the latter, the maid can be praised at the next staff meeting, so that others may appreciate the value of better guest relations. Realizing that continuous occupancy of any room causes additional wear and tear of the furnishings and may lead to personnel difficulties also, the room clerk should avoid selling rooms not yet made up instead of those already okay. When it is the only one meeting the guest's needs, he should be made aware of the fact that it is not yet ready for occupancy.

If a guest complains "I didn't sleep a wink last night, the bed was so uncomfortable," it is most helpful if he is asked "What was wrong, was the mattress too hard, or soft, bumpy, or what?" And also if he is staying another night. The mattress will be inspected, changed if not in good condition, but if only too hard or soft, it will be left on, if the same person is not using it, for the next morning's comment may well be "I've not had such a good night's sleep all the way across the country."

It will be much appreciated if the housekeeper is notified of guests who are ill, animals of any kind in rooms, those made up and re-occupied after the night maid left or any put out of order during the night, and for what reason; requests not to be disturbed or for early make up, as these aid in maid service. It should be standard practice for the room clerk to tell guests with an animal that the maid is not allowed to enter that room unless the guest is there or both are out. This has been proved to be a necessary safety measure.

Reservation Clerk

Notification of heavy occupancy ahead is most helpful to the house-keeper, as it warns against having too small a staff or too many rooms out of order at the stated time. In turn, the reservation clerk should be told of major renovation plans as soon as received so he can be prepared for a shortage of rooms on the dates named. If a reservation requests any thing extra or unusual, the housekeeper should know it.

Credit Manager

This manager expects to get daily light baggage reports and sleep-outs, as noted by maid's vacancy lists, and wants to know of excessive room or bar service and especially any attempt by the guest to borrow money from an employee.

Cashier

The cashier needs quick reports of any damages done in rooms—articles burned, broken or torn—so they can be put on the bill and collected for before the person leaves the hotel. The housekeeper should furnish her with a list of the prices to be charged for replacements. This list should be kept up to date.

Sales Department

The important sales department depends on the housekeeper to carry out their agreements for convention or meeting set-ups with the extras agreed on. Complete co-operation is *imperative,* for failure to please means loss of return business from that group, its individual members, and other organizations to which the same people belong or which ask for recommendations. "No oral orders" is a "must" here to avoid any possibility of misunderstanding. All such orders should be in writing and signed by the sales manager.

The housekeeper should be notified of all arrangements made, *well in advance* so that everything needed may be in readiness and an adequate staff be fully informed of their duties. Notice of any change of plans is needed immediately to avoid last minute confusion. The sales department should have a list of all equipment on hand so that if any extra movie screens, loud speakers, etc. are needed their rental may be arranged ahead of time. If frequent rentals show the need for additional pieces, it should be called to the attention of the sales manager when discussing matters with him. The housekeeper is responsible for keeping all equipment in first class condition.

Banquet Manager or Maitre d'Hotel

The housekeeper should be informed of function requirements in time to provide the proper amount of linen, extra help to move furniture (possibly the piano), polish the floor, set up screens for motion pictures, and fill various other requirements. Sometimes these are indicated on the weekly function list. If so, any changes of plan must be sent her as soon as made. In many places, when the set-up is agreed on, the committee chairman signs it and is told that for any changes made after a certain date, there will be a labor charge. This prevents much last minute confusion and unnecessary work.

Room Service

It is customary for maids to put room service tables in the corridor if they have not been removed when the room is to be made up. Bus boys or waiters should remove them promptly to avoid the disorderly appearance caused by a number of them in the hall and possible theft of silver and linen. When extra chairs are needed for meals in rooms or suites, the linen room should be notified in time to get them there at, or before, the time needed, to prevent borrowing from corridor or vacant rooms. All torn or burned linen should be sent to the linen room, not to the laundry. Unused napery should also go there, not be left in the pantry closets, where it is not available for use and often gets soiled or mussed, and must be laundered before it can be used. This adds to laundry expense and shortens the life of the linen.

Accounting Department

This department needs the housekeeper's assistance in approving bills as soon as the goods are received and checked; in meeting payroll deadlines; in sending employees' contracts and discharges promptly and her co-operation in taking glass, china, silver, and linen inventories.

Purchasing Agent

Small houses may depend on each department head to order the various things needed, as approved by management, but in large operations a special department is necessary. Definite specifications are demanded by the purchasing agent as a guide. Specifications, according to Mr. Herbert K. Witzky, means "a complete and detailed description in writing, of exactly what is to be bought." He states that the value of the department depends on its executive's knowledge of the many factors governing economical purchasing. The amount of money to be spent is decided by the approved budget, storage space available, and what capital is to be tied up. This also governs the quantity purchased, while quality is determined by the type of house.

The wise housekeeper realizes that one whose sole responsibility is purchasing will be in touch with many reliable sources, keep abreast of market conditions, be aware of where new products are in use in similar places and by direct contact, discover their value before buying. Naturally she will expect to hear of these reports and be consulted about substitutes. Records, orders, the O.K., and checking of invoices are some of the other duties spared her. After delivery, the steward often stores cleaning and guest supplies, issuing them on order. It is customary to specify a day for sending an order in the morning and picking up the things in the afternoon. Housekeepers are careful to meet the conditions and in return appreciate being notified ahead of time of a possible shortage, so she can take emergency measures.

Uniform Service

These employees rightfully expect cleanliness in their lavatories, lockers, and rest rooms if taken care of by housekeeping, but they should not add to the work by littering the floor and leaving soiled uniforms around. The latter condition can be lessened by sending these to a place named so that the offender is discovered when going to get a clean uniform without the soiled for exchange.

Porters

The head porter should send requisitions to the housekeeping department at least a day ahead of time when beds are to be taken out and furniture rearranged. Also when a sample room is to be set up he should also advise the number of sample sheets needed. Temptation to "borrow" sheets from maids' carts is thus avoided. A separate storage place should be provided for sample room equipment —tables, hat stands, clothes racks, extra lamps, and, if possible, some extra chairs. Otherwise there are apt to be chairs taken from corridors or even vacant rooms if there are many functions going on at the same time.

Chief Engineer

Upon no one is the housekeeper more dependent for close co-operation than the chief engineer. He is usually in charge of the maintenance crew so she must call on him for carpenters, painters, plumbers, electricians, and in some cases, furniture polishers and upholsterers. Only by the combined planning of these two departments with the room clerk can the loss of room sales and the expense of idle workers be avoided. The authorized list of repairs, renovation, and redecorations made by the manager, engineer and housekeeper's semi-annual inspection tour is used as a basis for work to be done. Unnecessary expense and guest annoyance are kept at a minimum when combined efforts result in immediate repairs of leaky faucets, loose door knobs, squeaky hinges, defective locks, etc.

Notice from the engineer that equipment sent for repair cannot be done at once will aid the housekeeper in planning the work for a period of time without it. Careful training of employees in the use and care of equipment will lessen the amount of repair work needed. He should always be consulted about the purchase of any type of equipment he is expected to repair.

The engineer expects housekeeping aid in conserving heat, water, light and power by instructions to maids that the first three must be turned off when not needed and the latter by using back elevators as little as possible. When there is a standard size light bulb designated for use in different areas, the person who OK's the room must request a change back to the right size when a larger one is found in the room.

Laundry

Occasionally the laundry is under the supervision of the housekeeper or engineer, but usually there is a separate laundry manager. The housekeeper should be notified at once of any labor shortage or breakdown of machinery, so that emergency measures can be planned to keep service up to standard. Laundry work is easier when room linen is sent down promptly, with badly stained or soiled pieces kept separate and by an agreement on a schedule for certain pieces to be done on assigned days only—for example: uniforms, Tuesday; bedspreads, Thursday; curtains, Friday. When issuing new linens it should be according to pre-arranged plans. Housekeeping can be helped by receiving an even distribution of clean pieces, and by separation of torn, burned, or stained pieces before folding. The former to be sent separately to the linen room for mending and the latter held in the laundry until a convenient time for bleaching.

Receiving Department

Housekeeping is expected to send quickly for all articles addressed to it.

Lost and Found Department

Where it is the policy of the institution to return things to the finder, this department usually has charge of lost and found articles, but for good results it must have the close cooperation of all other departments. Definite instructions from management as to the routine is most desirable. When possible, anything found should be sent to the housekeeping department as soon as discovered. Otherwise a phone call made to describe it and give any circumstances which might help to find the owner. So often a call comes asking if something has been found—perhaps a long distance call—and it is awkward to ask the caller to held the phone while one investigates. There may be a request to call back, which is costly. It makes a very favorable impression if the answer is, "Yes, we have it. What do you wish done with it?" If the loss is reported before the article is turned in, all details that would help identify it should be requested along with directions for mailing. If not found, there should be a notice of this sent at once.

If found at night after the linen room is closed, it is left at a designated place (often the room clerk's desk), from which it is picked up in the morning by the linen room attendant, when getting the keys. It should be properly marked with date, where and by whom found. If something valuable is turned in and is asked for by a guest who has returned to the hotel, it is advisable to let the finder deliver it when possible so as to get the reward or, if there is none, to know personally about it.

Lost and Found Storage

The cabinet illustrated here is a convenient way to store the things left behind. Each cubicle in the cabinet is marked for a different day of the month—1 through 31 with a large open space at the bottom for large packages. The articles found anywhere in the house on a certain day are put in the section marked for that date, to be held for 60 to 90 days, as required by the local statute. A record book is kept in duplicate giving the necessary information. This needs plenty of room for detailed description. These books can be bought already printed.

Number _____   Date _____

Where Found _____

Name of Finder _____

Description _____

_____

Delivered to _____

Date Delivered _____

By Whom _____

The completed original is fastened to the package before putting it away and the duplicate remains in the book.

Upon inquiry for a lost article, the book is consulted for a record on or near the date mentioned. If found, the package is easily located

Illustration shows Lost and Found Cabinet with each cubicle marked for a different day of the month. For full description see preceding page.

in the section under that date. The description is most important as many times the incorrect room number or date is given. A search through adjoining pages may show an article matching the description. If not, it is necessary to consult the guest's record card to discover in what room and on what date it was left. This may be due to a room clerk's carelessness in not notifying this department of a change of rooms so any article found in the room left could be sent to the new one instead of to Lost and Found.

When possible a space should be left behind the cabinet with a rod for hanging coats, suits, dresses, and hooked canes or umbrellas. A shelf above will take care of hats.

Personnel Department

It is advisable for the large establishment to assign here the responsibility for recruiting and screening applicants for all departments, but each department head is necessarily the one to make the final decision on hiring. There must be a definite job analysis and specifications for each type of worker with health, educational and personality requirements and a statement of those places where a handicapped person can be used. This saves much time for busy executives as only those best fitted for the job are sent for an interview. There are places where a member of this department does the training also. In that case the one designated should have teaching ability and training, and also firsthand information about the whole process (gained by actual experience) in order to be able to show and explain the steps taken as well as to tell about them.

After a talk with the department head about a worker's decision to leave or a dismissal, there is an exit interview with a member of personnel. These records are important in determining any "sore spots" in the executive branch of the staff. Often union, and other difficulties are also taken care of by this division.

Foods Department

Some housekeepers find their greatest inter-departmental problem in the handling of linen by the various rooms serving food. Sometimes it is necessary to ask for a meeting of those in charge of these with the manager, the maitre d'hotel, housekeeper, and laundry manager to discuss these problems and seek a solution. Often this results in better understanding and therefore closer cooperation.

Here is the report of one such meeting:

Question by housekeeper: "Why requisition so much more linen than required by the function list? Yesterday it stated 'Lunch for 100' but you asked for 175 napkins and 25 more cloths and no clean ones were returned."

Reply by captain in charge: "Because the reservations went up to 120 and guests always drop some napkins. Also we use them for other things. We sometimes find cloths with burns, holes or stains that cannot be used, so we always ask for more to save a second trip to the linen room."

Result: The captain agreed to try a 10% extra coverage in both napkins and cloths and to return those not used and any not usable to the linen room for repair instead of sending them to the laundry.

The laundry manager promised more care in separating torn and burned pieces before folding. He showed a large number of 22 and 18 inch napkins received so badly stained that bleaching was not effective. It was evident the stains had been made by wiping metal trays, walking on linen which had been dropped on wet concrete, leaving colored paper cups and decorations in the hamper with wet linen, wiping up spilled food from concrete floor and even using linen napkins to polish shoes. He also spoke of the delay for sorting caused by throwing soiled table linen down the chute from the ball-room floor, and asked to have linen sent to laundry immediately after each meal instead of holding that from breakfast till after lunch.

The housekeeper spoke of clean, unused linen left in drawers and on closet shelves in private dining rooms, probably by busboys in a hurry to get off duty. As no one else knew of them, it might cause a shortage for use elsewhere, they would also become dusty and need an extra laundering, or might be stolen.

At the end of the conference the following agreement was drawn up, each person present to receive a copy and a meeting was scheduled for a month later to see how the plan worked.

1. Drop boxes put at exit doors of all rooms serving food.

2. Small amounts of linen to be taken on trays to avoid wrinkling or soiling under arms; never piled on ballroom floor while waiting for tables to be set up; care used to avoid dropping on concrete; only dyed cloths used to wipe metal trays.

3. Only 10% increase in linen requisition over confirmed guest list.

4. All torn or burned linen sent to linen room; stained linen to laundry.

5. No table linen sent down chute.

6. Soiled table linen sent to laundry immediately after breakfast and lunch. That from dinner and supper sent there in locked hamper at close of rooms.

7. All colored debris shaken from table linen before placing it in truck. Pieces on which wine, tea, coffee, chocolate or ketchup was spilled to be separated from the rest.

8. Every employee requested to pick up misplaced table linen and send to laundry or linen room.

At the next meeting a big improvement was reported in both linen conservation and inter-departmental accord. About once a year such a meeting was called and any difficulties ironed out. The plan was so successful that it was adopted for other friction areas.

We have noted the relation of housekeeping with practically every other department and a few of the ways in which there can be greater co-ordination. You can of course think of many others from your own experience. Do not forget that the best plans will fail unless *attitudes* are right and that is the big problem.

Inter-Departmental Morale

Like all conditions in every sort of institution, smooth inter-departmental relations begin with top management, so definite specifications for their co-ordination should be worked out with the assistance of department heads. Where this has been done it has proved most effective in preventing friction and increasing effective operation. Such harmonious relations encourage understanding of each other's problems, a feeling of respect for the other person's point of view and willingness to discuss common difficulties, in the attempt to find a mutually advantageous solution. This leads to a willingness to change a procedure not working well in one place for another which will increase the efficiency of the whole organization. This is what is meant by being a part of the "Management Team," so desirable for satisfactory operation of our type of business. Adaptability and a sense of humor plus the good old "Golden Rule" all help. Someone has said "The machinery of human affairs needs the oil of good will to keep it running smoothly." Nowhere is this truer than in the large institution.

CHAPTER 5

The Housekeeper's Responsibilities to Her Staff

Finally, let us consider the housekeeper's responsibilities to her staff. We have already indicated some of these and others will be mentioned in detail later but the following are essential for achieving required results.

1. Recruiting for definite jobs according to specifications.

2. Careful screening and orientation.

3. Excellent basic training and continuous retraining to achieve the highest standard of work.

4. Making sure that immediate supervision is strict but kind.

5. Supplying attractive, well-fitting uniforms and the best working conditions possible—clean, cheerful lunch and rest rooms, toilet facilities, and locker rooms.

6. Furnishing adequate up-to-date equipment and work methods.

7. Increasing employee job satisfaction by impressing them with the value to their institution of their ability to please the guests.

8. Encouragement and praise when they do satisfy those they serve.

9. Training all capable and ambitious workers for the next step up to higher positions, making sure to have at least two preparing for all supervisory jobs to be used as relief workers, both regular and for emergencies.

10. The expression of appreciation for earnest effort and work well done in staff meetings, so that others may be stimulated to do the same.

11. Treating all employees in the same fair way so that they may all expect a "square deal."

12. Setting an example of dignity, calmness, and courtesy to every-

one—teaching them that these qualities bring personal satisfaction and popularity with both guests and fellow employees.

13. Showing sincere interest in their personal lives and problems when it appears they would welcome such interest.

14. Encourage any interest in learning because it tends to increase personal satisfaction and usually more effective work.

15. Building up ego by asking for suggestions in solving problems concerning their own working conditions or methods. Consider these carefully, and when not feasible, explain why.

These are just a few of the suggestions the housekeepers try to follow in order to inspire their staff members to greater usefulness and fuller and more satisfactory lives.

Part II

EMPLOYEES

CHAPTER 6

Recruiting

The locality and labor conditions largely govern the ways of getting new employees. When it is possible to transfer or promote present workers, this policy of advancement is an effective stimulant to good work.

Through Other Employees

First, a notice of the type of help needed should be posted on the linen room bulletin board. If this is not effective, place a notice on the board near the time keeper's station, where those in other departments can see it. Often this brings in excellent applicants and there are several advantages to this method:

1. Employees will recommend only those they expect will prove a credit to them.
2. They feel responsible for seeing that the newcomer likes the job and the other workers, so they do all they can to help bring this about.
3. The new employee wants to please the sponsor and tries to learn quickly and do good work.
4. It helps the morale of workers to realize they have a part in choosing new helpers.

The housekeeper should make a point of mentioning at a staff meeting that she is grateful to _____ for recommending _____ (the new employee) who is proving satisfactory. This should be done after the training has proved the new employee to be desirable.

If there is a union, the new person must be approved by the proper representative, unless already a member of the same Local. Except in times of surplus labor, the union is not often able to fill the job and is glad to get a new member.

Through the U. S. Employment Office

Definite qualifications must be furnished this office for each type of job as it is open. Otherwise, they may not be as careful as they should be in screening applicants, thus wasting the housekeeper's time. It is sometimes wise to ask the interviewer for lunch and a trip around working places so he can see the type of person needed.

Through Other Institutions

Occasionally applicants can be contacted through co-operative arrangement with other institutions where, at times, good workers are obliged to be dismissed through an unfortunate incident not really their fault. Occasionally a good employee who left because of illness or family troubles can be persuaded to return. Sometimes there may be the record of a likely prospect from among those who applied when there was no opening.

Local Workers

Resorts and small town institutions often depend on local residents for staffing. They usually take real interest in their local hotel or hospital and take real pride in their work. A small city institution often gets similar reactions from neighborhood people. These may be married women wishing to supplement their husband's wages for some special objective—a new home, to pay hospital bills, a car, or whatever it may be. Such people are good investments for they appreciate the chance to work and are conscientious about doing it acceptably. Often part-time employees may be found among them for rush periods or in cases of absenteeism.

The "help wanted" column of local newspapers is not often satisfactory as this way seems to attract the "floaters" or even more undesirable types. It is, however, a good way to get replacements for upholsterers, drapery makers, or cabinet men. Though pay in the latter cases is not as high as that in a private workshop, it is steady and not seasonal.

Student Help

Summer resorts often find college or high school students the answer for a few jobs, especially when they plan to take or are already in Institutional Management courses. Most colleges that offer such courses require a certain amount of on-the-job training, so these workers are usually of top value. They are in great demand and applications must be sent in early.

Physical Examinations

Most large institutions of all kinds provide a pre-employment physical examination to discover any ailment that might handicap a worker, lead to an accident, or result in illness. If the place is not large enough for a full-time doctor to be in attendance, a local clinic or young physician just getting started may be available. The complete information thus obtained becomes a part of an employee's work record.

Discovering Handicaps

In the few places where there is no such policy of pre-examination, the personnel department or the housekeeper must try to spot conditions which might hinder good work. During the interview, she will get an impression of general good health or the lack of it and a few simple tests can be made unobtrusively, as follows:

Hearing: It is a distinct handicap for a worker, coming in direct contact with guests to be even slightly deaf, but it may even be an asset for a seamstress or laundry worker. One question asked in a low tone usually shows up this disadvantage.

Sight: Filling out the application blank will indicate poor vision by the tendency to bend closely over it. It also shows how well the applicant can read and write and the slowness or speed in understanding. Careless writing may be due to nervousness or it may show all-around poor workmanship, depending on other test results.

Foot and Leg Conditions: Many housekeeping duties demand standing and walking so varicose veins, fallen arches, bad corns, bunions, or calluses are truly hampering. With women there will be a chance to notice any such serious conditions by sending them across the room to raise or lower a shade or on a similar errand. This often shows foot trouble by the kind of shoe worn.

Agility: Any object dropped will be a good way to see if bending is an effort and also if there is an instinctive helpful attitude. Usually a person of medium height can do the work needed more easily than one very tall because the latter is apt to develop a back ache from bending over the many studio beds now in use. The very short ones cannot reach the high shelves or the shower rod to dust them.

Personality Requirements: Neatness or the lack of it is apparent at a glance, as untidy hair, a soiled blouse or dress, excessive makeup, a stocking run, or shoes in need of attention. Hands and nails show when writing and bad breath or body odor is usually apparent. An agreeable voice, pleasant manner and good disposition, or the opposite is indicated in answers to why changes in jobs were made. A bad tempered individual is *never* a good employee in this work.

The application must show a clear picture of working history in the same or other occupations. The applicant should give the name of at least the last three places of employment with the time employed in each and the reasons for leaving, the pay received, other skills, and if any, other languages spoken, nationality, age, marital status, number of dependents. Attached to this information should be the requests for references. Nationality and languages spoken are increasingly important as foreign trade develops.

Most housekeeping workers come in close touch with guests daily, so their appearance, manners, intelligence, and attitudes are most important. They can do a first class selling job for the hotel or they can irritate the guest right out of the place, never to return. Unfortunately, there are no perfect employees so one must take the best applicants available and be prepared to help him overcome their faults through training procedures.

CHAPTER 7

Hiring and Orientation

Except in an emergency, there will be intervals between the first interview and actual hiring in order to check references as to honesty, dependability, and other necessary qualities. Careful selection is the first important step toward having an efficient staff, low turnover, and a minimum payroll. If the employee's replies are satisfactory, the doctor's examination takes place. If this is acceptable the applicant is ready for work.

Induction or Orientation Period

First, there is a conference with the executive housekeeper and an explanation of rules as to working hours, meals, pay days, days off, vacation, furnishing and laundering uniforms, and many other things. Fringe benefits are mentioned and pay deductions discussed, along with pension funds, credit union or bonuses, employee publications, and possible discount from street floor stores. There is emphasis placed on everyone's responsibility for keeping safety rules to avoid accidents and fires. The fact is stressed that their superiors (supervisors or the housekeeper) are always willing to talk over anything that troubles the new employee.

Next comes the change into their uniforms after an introduction to the linen room attendant and the new employee's instructor. If the latter is an inspectress, she takes the newcomer to the manager's office and introduces her to the "boss" who welcomes her and presents her with a copy of the House Manual. Next comes a tour through the house which means a trip through those public rooms which are not engaged at the time, through a sample suite, and the various offices and work shops. Where possible, an introduction is made to the person in charge in each place. These visits to all parts of the institution are greatly appreciated as it gives the new person a real understanding of the size and beauty of the establishment and a feeling of being really a part of the force. At lunchtime, another employee takes her to the lunchroom or cafeteria and sees that she meets some fellow workers. After lunch she is guided back to the linen room to meet the instructress and go to a room to start learning.

Printed Instructions

The House Manual given by the manager gives information of all kinds needed by every employee, but there must also be a special supplement which adds the particular instruction for each department with one section "For the Newcomer." This is sometimes given out by the housekeeper at the close of the first day. It should contain at least the following with all figures written in for each individual:

1. Starting wage—if paid by hour, day, or week.
2. Date of first pay day and where and at what hour to get it.
3. If paid by cash or check. If the latter, where it can be cashed.
4. How much is withheld and for what purpose.
5. Amount of take-home pay.

Following are the printed instructions handed out with the Manual by one large hotel to all new housekeeping employees. They may serve as a guide for others.

1. Having passed our doctor's examination before signing the contract, we want you to know there is a nurse on duty in Room＿＿＿ on the ＿＿＿ floor from 10 A.M. to 5 P.M., Monday through Friday to take care of accidents or injury of any kind no matter how slight. When necessary, she will make arrangements for an office visit or call the doctor in case of major injuries. When the nurse is off duty, go to your first aid station for help. If necessary, the assistant manager will send you to a doctor or a hospital in a cab.

2. Every housekeeping employee is hired as a "relief worker" to be used as often as possible after training and to be put on a full time schedule at the end of two weeks, if not sooner.

3. Instruction in our methods of work is given by a well qualified trainer, who receives, as a teaching bonus, one extra day's pay for the

first two days with you, and the new employee gets one day's pay for the same time.

4. Regular weekday hours of day employees in this department are from 8 A.M. to 4 P.M. and 9 A.M. to 5 P.M. on Sundays and holidays, with one-half hour for a self-service lunch in the cafeteria (or lunchroom).

5. Night workers are on duty from 4 P.M. to midnight with one-half hour for supper. They also come in a half hour later on Sundays and holidays. All food must be eaten in the lunch room and never taken to guest room floors.

6. Employees use only the rear entrance and elevators. They *always* stamp the time clock when going in or out. If obliged to leave the establishment during working hours, they must first get permission from the housekeeper or her assistant, and leave their keys in her office to pick up on the way back to the floor.

7. An employee obliged to stay out because of illness or family affairs must notify the linen room as far in advance of reporting for work as possible, explaining why absence is necessary and when the return to duty may be expected.

8. Blue Cross and Blue Shield Insurance are, in many cases, paid by the institution and if the preceding employee's coverage included the family, that will also be taken care of.

9. Employees are given one week's vacation after one year, 10 days after two years, and two weeks after three years of employment. Vacation periods are assigned according to seniority.

10. Whenever possible, the department head will arrange for extra time off if the employee wants to take it at her own expense.

11. When every bed in the assigned section is used and cots are put in, maids are paid extra. When any rooms are vacant, the maids are expected to dust the vacant ones and take care of others elsewhere as requested. When some maid is absent and there is no relief, those who wish may take care of extra rooms and get extra pay for it. No one is obliged to do this but it is appreciated.

12. Each night maid is assigned to three floors but is expected to help elsewhere as needed. If a sudden storm comes up, all personnel are expected to help close the windows in public rooms and in those where guests are out.

13. All housemen are hired for general work when and where needed. They may be assigned a certain regular job but are expected to do whatever is asked of them by the department head. Orders for them are received from the linen room and reports are made there when the job is completed.

14. Every employee is required to report any unusual happening to the floor inspectress at once.

CHAPTER 8

Job Analysis and Supervision

Satisfactory work and a minimum payroll are objectives toward which all executive housekeepers must aim unceasingly. Proper selection and induction of employees are the first steps toward this goal. But analysis as to what is to be done and specifications as to the required way to do it must precede the next objective—thorough training. This breakdown into details of the job helps both teacher and pupil by providing both with a "blue print," which is quite as valuable to the small as to the large house. The following form is approved by the National Executive Housekeepers' Association:

Job Analysis

1. *Department*
   Executive
   Immediate supervisor
   Time for training
      inexperienced
   Time for training
      experienced
   Immediate position leading
      to present one
   Position growing out of
      present one
   Contacts
   Sources of supply
   Hours on duty
   Total weekly hours
   Days off
   Responsibilities
   Maintenance
   Tools used
   Accident hazards

2. *Type of Employee*
   Sex and marital status
   Nationality

   Age limits

   Member of union

   Education

   Experience
   Physical qualifications
   Mental qualifications
   Emotional qualifications
   Other qualifications
   Description of job
   Working conditions
   Wages, how and when paid
   Vacation
   Sick leave

This may be varied to meet conditions of course.

Job Description for Vacuum Man
Schedule of Duties

At 8 A.M., report to the linen room in uniform to get special orders and any equipment left there for repair.

Get clean dust cloth, then go to assigned floor.

Pick up vacuum hose and attachments, radiator brush, long handled duster, and step ladder.

Be careful in use of ladder to avoid falls, and in picking up broken glass to prevent serious cuts.

Start with checkouts, if any, then vacant rooms, and those where guests are out. Except in air-conditioned rooms, open windows while working, except in stormy or windy weather.

Always leave door open during your work, but be sure to close it when finished, and if occupied, see that it is locked by maid.

Clean the closet light, high rod, and shelves.

In the room, do high dusting, ceiling, lights, draperies, cornices, venetian blinds, and window screens.

Move all furniture away from walls, dust the back of each piece, wall, moldings, and mopboards. Vacuum carpet before replacing furniture exactly where it belongs. Start at point farthest from door and work toward it.

Dust both sides of all doors and the transom, and report it if it needs repair or oiling.

Report damage to furniture or fixtures to the linen room or inspectress at once.

You are responsible for the heavy cleaning of all rooms on the three floors assigned to you, each one to be serviced within each ten days.

Corridors are to be vacuumed in turn or as necessary between times.

CHAPTER 9

Training

There must be a well-planned system for proper training which aims at teaching the best, easiest, and quickest way of doing each part of the work so thoroughly that, with supervised practice, the actions become almost involuntary. Such perfection is seldom attained but trying for it always brings better results than any lesser attempts —nearer to the high standard of quality desired. Work habits will be only as good as basic training has been and as the supervisor demands. Thus, the choice of an instructor is all-important. The administrative duties of the executive housekeeper in a large institution are such that she is not able to give the time to teaching the individual workers. It is her duty to choose someone with the right qualifications or potentialities to be trained by her in the necessary teaching techniques. This person may be the first assistant, inspectress, a maid, or a member of the personnel department. All must be given definite instruction and practice in approved techniques of each phase of the work until she can do it to the satisfaction of the housekeeper and then be coached in teaching procedures until there is no doubt she is capable of instructing others. If a maid is selected, it should be someone with leadership qualifications, whose excellent work record is acknowledged by the other maids with whom she is popular. Such a person has a good influence on her associates and the newcomers as well.

The American Hotel Institute card on Job Instruction says: "The learner can perform *if* the instructor has taught." Let us see what some of the faults might be if performance is not up to standard.

1. *Telling* without *showing* how the work should be done.
2. Giving no chance for the pupil to *tell* and *show*.
3. Omitting some required steps.

4. Talking too fast.
5. Using words not familiar to the pupil.
6. Telling too much at one time.
7. Giving no chance for the pupil to ask questions.
8. Getting impatient.
9. Stopping the lesson too soon.
10. Not continuing supervision, encouragement, and correction of faults after the pupil goes on regular duty.

It is important to introduce the pupil to the teacher in a way that shows the confidence of the housekeeper in the instructor, for her encouragement and to give the learner faith in the teacher's ability. Also, to make her feel that she really can do the work right after she is shown how and that she, too, will be praised when she deserves it.

Preparation of the trainee includes making her feel at ease, explaining why the methods are different from those she uses at home, that she can learn the new ways as well as anyone else and must *always* do as she has been taught.

The Trainee's First Day

This is always the hardest time so much encouragement is needed. Try to train only in checkouts the first day.

We learn by the use of our senses and psychologists tell us that the more senses used in the process, the quicker we learn. Correct training therefore, starts with a demonstration of how the work is done—*Seeing*. Next comes the explanation of why it is done that way—*Hearing*. Questions are encouraged and the showing and telling are repeated until the trainee seems to understand. Then she is asked to do the task herself, thus using the sense of *Touch*, explaining at each step shows up wrong ideas and corrections can be made at once.

The teacher must go slowly, speak clearly, and correct patiently, remind and encourage the pupil until sure the lesson has been well learned. It is a good idea, at the end of the first day, for the trainee to stop in the housekeeper's office on the way out. Meanwhile the trainor has advised the housekeeper of any physical difficulties which may have shown up and reports on attitudes and aptitudes of the trainee. A few words of encouragement will give her a feeling of being liked and needed. Then another maid from the floor is asked to show her the way out. It often gives the old-timer an interest in the newcomer, resulting in a new acquaintance.

As teacher and trainee go from room to room to work for the first time in occupied rooms, there will be some variations in method caused by the guest's preferences. This is valuable to show how rules must be adapted to a guest's wants without lowering work standards. This is a chance to emphasize the need for keeping guests contented and the loss of income if this is not done; to explain that these are the people who really pay the wages, so they are the most important people in the house.

Trainee as Relief Maid

When the trainee is capable of working alone, she is often assigned as relief maid on the floor on which she trained because this is familiar ground and she knows the other maids. If possible, the teacher is her inspectress that first day and should introduce her to the person who will supervise her work next. Naturally this inspectress will continue to encourage her but must call her attention to anything forgotten or not done correctly. Kind firmness is necessary right from the start to prove that there is no chance for poor work. The first day on a new floor under a new inspectress is trying, but if treated with tact her interest in the job and confidence in being able to do it will increase. At the second day's conference with the housekeeper, the trainee will be asked if there is anything not clear in the Manual or work specifications and explanations for these matters are given. If there is available a "Maids' Alphabet" or a "Do and Don't" sheet it may be given then as it will have more meaning than it would have earlier. "Why don't you look it over tonight and mark what is not clear so we can talk about it tomorrow?" is one way of getting it read. The next consultation may be delayed until there is time for giving instruction on the necessity for personal cleanliness, good grooming, and courteous treatment of everyone with whom she comes in contact; of doing an honest day's work; the importance of housekeeping service and how she can help make the institution a success by obeying rules and having the right attitude toward guests.

In some large hospitals and colleges where several are to be trained at one time, a classroom is set up the same as the rooms to be serviced. In this room is a blackboard, cabinets for all sorts of things used in the building, and a closet for samples of all approved cleaning materials in use. Standard equipment is brought in for demonstration. Also a plan of the housekeeping chart with its relation to all other departments, posters on accident and fire prevention, and visual aids for grooming and other matters. These all add interest to lessons. Such a place is just right for staff meetings with the posters changed each time. If necessary to teach an entire class as happens when opening a new house or in times of full occupancy when short handed, it would be a great help.

Employees get careless if supervision is not kind, yet firm and constant and must be brought back to standard. Retraining would be easier ín such a place as that mentioned above. It will be less difficult if done carefully, one point at a time, with explanations of how the work will be easier if done correctly. A bit of praise makes the person *want* to improve more than a scolding will. "Anyone who makes such a good bed" or "who cleans a bath so beautifully" or whatever they do well will encourage better work in most cases.

Safety Training

An analysis of hotel accidents shows that about 50% occur in the housekeeping department so effective instruction in accident prevention and in the development of safety consciousness is evidently lacking. Many institutions find that a Safety Committee formed of representatives from every department helps by making employees realize that the reduction of casualties belongs to every single worker in the house. When chosen by their fellows to serve on such a committee for a month, given a sizeable safety button, which they keep, and urged to make suggestions for new ways to prevent accidents, it increases safety consciousness and in time, everyone who has been on the committee becomes eager to win the City Hotel or Hospital Association Safety Award for the year.

Every possible means of decreasing accidents is of value from the humanitarian standpoint and also because it will reduce insurance premiums. Research has established the fact that all accidents are caused by either a hazardous condition or a person's careless or unsafe action or both. To prevent them requires wide-awake scrutiny of property to rectify at once situations tending to cause the former and for the latter, careful personnel training. There are many aids to planning an accident-prevention campaign offered by those insurance companies that specialize in Employee Liability insurance. Any insurance company will give expert aid in planning an effective program including speakers, manuals, posters, still films, possibly movies.

Fire prevention is also an ever-present problem. How can we combat smoking in bed by the careless guest? and throwing hot matches in the waste baskets or on the floor? Here again, training in fire prevention and the planning and organization of emergency measures to be taken for their control in case they do occur are the responsibility of all department heads, under the general direction of top management. Your city fire department is happy to aid this effort, especially in large cities where one person is usually given this assignment. Insurance companies are also equipped to help with suggestions for training. This matter is so important that it should be a definite part of the training program.

CHART OF HOUSEKEEPING DEPARTMENT

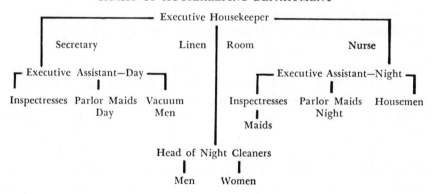

This chart is for a large house. In a smaller place there probably would be no nurse, no night inspectress and only one day inspectress. Sometimes the housekeeper has drapery makers, upholsterers, and furniture finishers on her payroll. In others there may be painters and paper hangers also. Other operations include all these workers in the maintenance department.

CHAPTER 10

Procedures

Since procedures also vary with every type of institution, the examples given here must be modified to meet each special case. They may, however, stimulate thinking. The executive housekeeper in a large institution needs a first assistant to relieve her of much routine supervision so that her time can be spent in planning work methods, consultation with management, other department heads, guests, employees, and often salesmen.

First or Executive Assistant Housekeeper

This person is her next in command and takes her place when necessary. She should have qualifications for advancement to the top position, when adequately trained. She is in charge of all inspectresses, of guest rooms, suites, public rooms and lobby; of the linen room workers, sometimes the payroll, the lost and found department and she answers the telephone if the house is not large enough to have a secretary for the housekeeper.

It is her duty to bring to the immediate attention of her superior any deviation from regular routine. There should be a definite outline of her responsibilities to avoid errors and confusion. She must know *what* is to be done, *who* is to do it, *how* the order is to be carried out and *when* it must be completed. Her responsibility should carry corresponding authority if she is to work effectively. In *no* case should she be criticized in the presence of other employees. There much be harmonious relations between the housekeeper and her assistant if the department is to run smoothly and effectively. All workers must be aware of her authority.

Night Housekeeper

This person is really another first assistant who takes the burden of supervising the night staff. She must be a mature person with plenty of common sense and good judgment as her authority must be recognized by all night employees. She, too, should have the qualifications for the executive housekeeper's position after some daytime experience. Her hours are usually from 4 P.M. to midnight with two consecutive days off and she has the privilege of eating in an assigned public dining room at a definite hour.

A conference with her superior is scheduled for 4 P.M. daily and a telephone call at any time can reach her in case of emergency before she goes home. She leaves a report of any unsatisfactory conditions, etc., for the morning.

Inspectors, Supervisors or Floor Housekeepers

Either title is used for the person who supervises all workers in bedrooms, suites, corridors, elevator spaces and stairways in her assigned section. She reports for work at 8 A.M. on weekdays and 9 A.M. on Sundays and holidays; goes to lunch in the assigned dining room at 11:30 to avoid the 12 o'clock rush; has two consecutive days off each week and takes her turn on holidays. It is her duty to see that all cleaning is done properly as scheduled and according to approved procedures. If management does not furnish uniforms for her, she is expected to wear simple dark dresses in winter and lighter ones in summer if she wishes. No conspicuous jewelry is allowed. She must be refined in manner and speech, as an example to employees and a credit to the institution, in her relations with guests.

Typed instructions in full detail are as necessary for these people as for those they direct. Often a request for their job outline will show the details they are apt to neglect. It is a good idea to have them outline their routine in this way, to see where they may need retraining. It also gives the housekeeper a chance for impressing on them the increased emphasis placed on their work and the great value of their contribution to the success of the establishment. Their task is not easy and a pat on the back at the end of a hard day helps a great deal.

Procedures for Putting Rooms Out of Order

When the inspectress reports a room in bad condition, it is examined by the housekeeper or her first assistant and the head painter to decide if it should be a wash and touch-up job or if it needs a new coat of paint. When the latter, the color is at once decided upon and samples submitted to the executive housekeeper or outside decorator. The latter would of course also decide on color and kind of carpet, bedspreads, draperies, and all accessories. She will either give necessary directions to the shops involved or take care of them outside. Meanwhile management decides if new furniture is needed. If so, its delivery is ordered from manufacturer or storehouse.

The room clerk puts the room out of order and work begins. First, the inspectress lists repairs needed; mirrors to be changed; metal fittings to be refinished; frayed telephone cord or damaged mouthpiece replaced; radiators or plumbing that need attention, etc. This list is given to the first assistant, who then checks to be sure nothing has been omitted before sending orders to the shops.

The room is then stripped by the maid, who removes linen from beds and bath; puts soiled linen down the chute; and in case of unused linen, puts it elsewhere. When new furniture is planned, all supplies are taken from desk, dresser drawers, and closet to be stored until needed. Housemen trained for this work remove pictures, draperies, venetian blinds, wall mirrors, lamps, telephone books, ashtrays, and pillows. These are all taken to the places directed—the blinds to be washed, painted, and retaped—the shades and draperies to the proper shop for cleaning—the pictures and mirrors to be stored—other furnishings shown to the first assistant housekeeper for directions as to where they should go. The upholsterer takes chairs to his shop for cleaning and use in another room or for recovering, unless new are to be used. The carpenter takes door mirrors and any metal fixtures to be refinished and inspects furniture for repairs. Engineer's men remove ceiling lights, check wires, plumbing, radiator and either make repairs there or take elsewhere. Carpet man removes the old carpet to make over for a smaller room, after which the walls can be prepared for painting. Before painting is begun, the telephone wires are covered with paper and a fitted plywood or other type cover is put over the tub to prevent paint spatters.

If the same furniture and carpet are to be used, the houseman places the furniture where the painter says it will not interfere with the work. If the room has twin beds, one is left standing, spring and mattress of the other placed on top with foot and head boards (if any), side boards, and slats then covered carefully. If the same pictures and wall mirrors will be used again, they can be turned upside down on the bed with lamp shades, and the whole covered. A sign saying, "Glass, do not put anything here" is needed. Several of these should be on hand for use as wanted. Of course, the carpet must be properly protected with dropcloths.

It is a good rule to follow a telephone conversation with these other departments with a typewritten copy of orders given or decisions made. If there is no list of all possible work to be done by all departments, you can make out your own and have them multigraphed. They act as insurance against misunderstandings. Here are two examples:

Housekeeper to Room Clerk
        Date _____ Time _____ Room number _____
Please put Room _____ out of order for the following reasons.
Wash and touch up. Carpet washing. Window washing.
Leaky radiator. Furniture polishing (or cleaning).
Changing draperies.
Signed _____

Housekeeper to Engineer
        Date _____ Time _____ Room number _____
Complete paint job. Bad bath and door mirrors.
Loose towel bar and shower rod. Noisy radiator.
Refinish bath and door fixtures. Two broken window panes.
Signed _____

PROCEDURES FOR PUTTING ROOM BACK IN ORDER

When all work is completed, the inspectress makes sure it is satisfactory, then supervises getting it ready for sale as soon as possible. This is one institution's procedure. Be sure any paint spots are removed from window panes, bath tiles, floor, fixtures, and outside of tub, toilet bowl and fixtures. The maid then cleans the bathroom thoroughly, as instructed, puts in all supplies according to standard, closes the door, and puts a "Do no disturb" sign on the knob as a warning for other workers. She cleans the closet next, sees that rods and hooks are free from paint spots and polished, wipes the shelf and floor, cleans door mirror, sets the closet up to standard and closes the door, using another sign on the knob.

Other workers, meanwhile, are washing outside sills and windows, replacing venetian blinds or shades, ceiling lights, transom rods, polishing furniture, and cleaning up any debris before the carpet is laid, if new, or washed and vacuumed, if not. When the carpet is ready, springs and mattresses are vacuumed, the beds put in place and made. Draperies, mirrors, and pictures are hung, lamps cleaned and connected. Furniture is replaced and polished, desk and other drawers set up to standard, wastebasket and accessories placed where they belong. When all is ready, the inspectress checks everything and tells the room clerk the room is ready for sale.

Standard Room Set-Up

This set-up varies widely with the size and type of institution. A copy is usually framed and kept in the maid's closet for reference. This is a sample of the set-up in one of the large chain hotels.

Bathroom:

Rug on floor.
Bath mat placed over edge of tub on top of rubber mat.
Soap: 3 cakes—one for tub, one for basin, one in cabinet.
Towels:
Single room—2 face, 2 bath, 3 face cloths.
Double bed—3 face, 3 bath, 3 face cloths or 2 of each and 3 hand towels.
Twin beds—4 face, 4 bath, 4 face cloths or 3 of each and 4 hand towels.
Suite—4 hand, 4 bath, 4 face, 4 face cloths and 4 hand towels.
Water glasses—2 on lower shelf of cabinet or on open shelf under it.
Tissue dispenser.
Shoe cloth.
Toilet paper: 1 in holder; ½ package in cabinet.

Closet:

"Do Not Disturb" Card on room side of closet door.
Clothes hangers—4 each of men's and ladies' (wooden), 4 extra metal hangers.

Laundry bags—2 on shelf with lists attached.
Valet Notice—on hook near door.

As glass tops are so seldom used, notices formerly put under them are now included in folder in desk drawer.

Dresser:

On top—current entertainment notice, radio, lamps, ashtray and matches.
Top drawer—Gideon Bible.
Lower drawer—extra blankets; 1 for double bed, 2 single for twin beds.

Desk:

Top—lamp, ashtray, matches.
Drawer—Telegraph blanks, floor plan showing fire exits, disaster directions. Folder containing all house information in one side and stationery in the other—6 sheets of paper and 6 envelopes if only one kind; 4 of each if both men's and ladies' sizes, 2 of each kind of postals, 1 blotter, 1 ball point pen.

Night Table:

Top—phone, ashtray and matches, possibly notice about ordering breakfast at night.
Shelf—Telephone directories.

General:

Baggage racks—at foot of bed unless a part of multi-use piece of furniture. 1 for large bed and other in closet, 1 at foot of each twin bed.
Waste basket beside desk.
Television so it is visible from both easy chair and bed.

PROCEDURE FOR MAID'S WORK

No manual yet written can be followed implicitly in all institutions, but everywhere the aim is the same—to achieve cleanliness, comfort and quiet for all patrons. No method can be completely successful unless followed faithfully every day, and without systematic routine, it is easy to forget something which is seldom overlooked by the guest. Here is one "blueprint for maids" used in a large hotel.

"Give your number to the timekeeper, stamp it, go to locker room, change into uniform, and go to linen room for key, supplies, and any special orders. Go to the section assigned you and be *very quiet,* as there may be many late sleepers. Take list of vacant rooms or those where people are out but do not try key in doors having *"Do not disturb"* sign or where night latch shows. If you hear voices, try key very softly as it may be guests are sleeping and radio or T.V. is on. If a room seems unoccupied, look in bath, closet and dresser drawers for personal belongings before marking it vacant on your list. Be sure to mark each room *exactly* as you find it as the front office depends on you for accurate information. If you find any thing unusual or out of order be sure to report it to the inspectress as she collects your vacancy list. If it is an emergency, call the housekeeper's office at once."

Making Up a Room

First stock your cart with all supplies needed to avoid unnecessary steps. Wheel it to the room, park it close and parallel with the wall, halfway across the open door, to be easy for you to reach the things needed and to prevent anyone else from taking anything. This is the only thing to be left in the corridor. All other working equipment must be taken into the room with you. Unless otherwise notified, you will start with checkouts in order to get them ready for sale as quickly as possible. Today the majority of institutions are air-conditioned. If the one in which you work is not, the first thing to do is to open the window to let the room air while you work. If windy or stormy, open it as much as you can with safety and comfort. Next, strip soiled linen from beds. Be sure to shake soiled linen over the bed to avoid breaking eyeglasses, dentures or a watch by dropping them on the floor or throwing them down the chute. Place in bag on your cart, bringing back the setup of clean linen with you. The sooner the soiled linen gets to the laundry, the better, so empty bag down the chute after making up three or four rooms depending on the number of pieces changed.

While beds and blankets are airing, clean the bath and closet in the way you have been taught and set them up as instructed. Before making beds, look around to see if anything has been left—in closet, behind bathroom door, in desk or dresser drawers, behind draperies, or under bed. If you find something, notify the Lost and Found Department immediately, as there might be a long distance call about

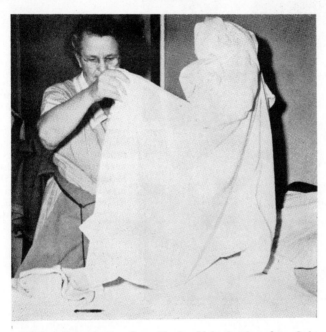

When beds are stripped, maids should be instructed to shake out the bedding to locate guests' articles which may be mixed in with the bed clothes.

it. Mark whatever you find with the room number, date, time, and your name and take to the linen room the next time you go there. If it is not called for, you will receive whatever you found in 60 or 90 days (according to local laws).

Empty wastebasket and dresser drawer onto a newspaper to see if anything valuable was left there in error and also to prevent cut fingers from broken glass or razor blades. Most wastebaskets have a fire and water resistant finish so there is no need for a paper lining, but they do need wiping out with a damp cloth. One method of fire prevention is to empty ash trays into a tin box kept on the cart for that purpose. When all trash is on the paper, roll it up and take it to the trash can on the service landing. Extra glasses, soiled dishes, and empty bottles are taken to the shelf on the back landing also.

When emptying waste baskets, maids should be instructed to empty them on a widely spread newspaper. This serves two purposes. First, it prevents the maids' hands being cut on razor blades or broken glasses which guests may have tossed into the waste basket. Second, belongings of the guests may have found their way into the basket by mistake. This method makes it easy to locate them.

Bed Making

When stripping bed you have noted any repairs needed on spring or mattress and they have been repaired or changed while you cleaned bath and closet. Never leave anything soiled for the use of a new check-in, so change bedpad if necessary. This is placed on the bed so it is the same distance from top and bottom and from side to side. The "One Trip Around" method of bed making is widely used because of the fewer steps necessary and the resulting lessened fatigue. This method is clearly described on the next page. Where given a fair trial it has proved so satisfactory that no one wants to go back to the old way.

How to Make a Bed "Once Around"

1. Place pad on bed equally distant from head, foot and two sides.
2. About a foot away from the center of the bed, grasp the first sheet with both hands and open with a sharp flip right side up, and with small hem at top of bed. From center of bed, spread sheet to the headboard and tuck under mattress. Miter corner at the head and tuck that under. Move to lower half of bed tucking first sheet under mattress and miter corner at foot of bed. Tuck at foot of bed.
3. Open and place second sheet on in same manner as the first sheet. Second sheet is to rest against headboard ready to turn over blanket if a third sheet is not used.
4. Spread blanket on to within 8″ of the headboard and turn second sheet over for protection unless another one is customary.
5. If third sheet is used to cover blanket, open it in the same way, right side up with wide hem at the top. Fold this over top of blanket and bring second sheet up over it halfway across the bed.
6. Miter corners and tuck second sheet, blanket and third sheet at foot of bed.
7. Move to other side starting at the head of bed. Lay back second sheet, blanket and third sheet. Tuck in first sheet under mattress. Miter corner and continue tucking in tightly to the foot. Second sheet, blanket and third sheet are not tucked in under sides but are left hanging or folded under lightly, so that they will not pull out under first sheet when the guest gets into bed.
8. Bed is now ready for putting pillow in place and spread on.
9. Arrange spread over pillow, and the job is done, without those many trips around the bed which are so tiring.

Use the electric broom or other tool to clean edges of carpet, under dresser and bed and in center of room, starting at right of door and going all the way around.

Use a treated duster on wooden or steel furniture, a damp one on plastic coverings, a soft untreated one on satin or other delicate upholstery, and (before dusting) a stiff brush on heavy or textured material. Check setup of desk and dresser drawers, and tops of desk, night table, and dresser. Adjust draperies and venetian blinds. When testing lights, see that lampshades have seams turned to wall. Stand at door, test ceiling and side lights and look all the way around the room to see if anything has been forgotten, then let the inspectress know it is ready for her O.K.

Making Up Occupied Rooms

Unless immediate service is requested, make up occupied rooms when guest is out. Here surface dusting is done, bath and bed linen changed, but bedspreads, shower sheet, floor and tub mats are not changed unless soiled or wrinkled. Dresser drawers are not opened, nor clothes in closet touched unless something has fallen or is left in an untidy way in the room, in which case it is hung up in the closet. Guest's personal belongings must be handled with great care when dusting and if anything is accidentally broken it must be reported immediately so that the housekeeper can see if the owner is willing to have it replaced and where it may be purchased. Usually the worker responsible has to pay for it. Do not touch written or type-written papers and if papers or magazines are on the floor, pick them up and put them on desk or table. Only what is left in the waste-basket can be thrown out. Shake out any wrapped-up towel to be sure no stockings or underwear are in it. Do the work as guest requests if the only change is in routine, but ask permission if it differs from your orders—making up the bed with same linen for instance. The inspectress will arrange things if there is a request for your service at a time when you are scheduled elsewhere. When a man wants his room made up while he is there, another maid will be asked to help you make it up quickly. Leave door ajar. When working with a lady in the room, the door may be closed if "Maid Working" sign is on door knob.

Any remarks about the hotel, good or bad, should be reported to the inspectress. Management will be told of it and decide if a bad impression can be changed or if the praise is to be acknowledged.

Making Up Permanent Guests' Rooms

This work is usually done at a regular hour. The care of such a room or apartment is more like that in a private home. Beds and bath linen are changed daily unless otherwise instructed, but dusting and other cleaning is much like that in occupied rooms. Vacuum man works at stated times and maid does the general cleaning before or after he is through as desired. Taking care of these guests' belongings is most important as they are often of great value. Time schedules and any change from regular service routine should be listed in maid's closet so relief maid will make no mistakes.

Care of Vacant Rooms

Dust these and flush toilets daily so they will be ready for occupancy when needed. Do this when not able to get into occupied rooms and check a (D) for dusted on your work list. You will be asked to do other work in the time not used for occupied rooms. This probably will be to care for rooms in another section or to help get a room out of or in order. It could be extra cleaning in your own section if rooms had been occupied by children or if cots were used.

End-of-Day Chores

When your rooms are finished see that your linen closet is neat and the floor clean, tidy up your cart and list supplies needed for the next day. Lock truck in closet. Change into your street clothes. Put out the lights. Take to the linen room your key, glass towel, list of needed supplies, lost and found articles, reports of rooms to be made up, and repairs not yet made. Ask the timekeeper for your card and punch your time going out.

PROCEDURE FOR NIGHT MAIDS

The hours are 4 P.M. to midnight with one-half hour for supper at the time and place scheduled. This maid must be right on time in order to start at once where the day maids have left off. Get a card from the timekeeper and after punching it, go to the linen room for keys, guest supplies (in aluminum basket for easy carrying from floor to floor), list of makeups, or special orders. When in uniform, start taking vacancies. The work is done in the same way as that of the day maid. Check outs are done first so that all rooms will be rentable as quickly as possible.

You are assigned to no certain floors but will be sent where occupancy demands. On a busy night, you may have to get a refill for your supply basket when going to supper. Get it on your way back to the floor to which you are then sent. Be very quiet after supper as many folks like to rest before going out or may be asleep. Do not try your key in any lock where the night latch shows, where the "Do Not Disturb" sign is on the knob, or you hear voices. *Always* knock before trying the key and if there is an answer, say "This is the night maid checking, please excuse." Put a question mark on your room list and return later. If the room appears vacant, look carefully, as instructed, for personal belongings before marking it vacant on your list. Otherwise someone might be put in an occupied room. Be sure to mark every room exactly as you find it as the room clerk depends on your check list to know what is saleable. Always follow instructions for "lost and found" articles.

Should the hall telephone ring, answer as quickly as possible to avoid disturbing guests and to save time of operator and linen room attendant, who may be trying to reach you. Many houses today have a light system of calling floor workers. Watch for that and follow instructions. Another way to contact employees is by means of the "walkie-talkie" system. This is proving most efficient.

Keep your eyes and ears open for any out-of-ordinary or suspicious actions. Report them at once to inspectress or linen room attendant. Management depends on *you* to help in keeping out undesirables and so retain the good name of the hotel. Get in touch with linen room, as directed, when your assigned work is done. Before leaving any floor, see that linen closet is in order, lights out, and door locked, as you may not be back there. At time designated, change into street clothes, and return key, glass towel, supply basket, and soiled apron to linen room, before checking out on timecard. Be sure to list any room which you were unable to enter.

Maids' Night Service

Usually this is not common practice for all guests except in luxury houses, but may be customary for suites, where there are couch beds, or on request. As it is not usually started till after 9 o'clock, there is time for taking vacancies, making up check-outs and attending to makeups, first. In rooms assigned for this service, knock on door quietly and if there is an answer, say "Night maid, at what time shall I come back to tidy your room?" Note time on night service list and return as soon after that as you can. If they do not want this attention, put "N" after room number. When there is no answer, enter very quietly as the occupant may be asleep. If no one is there and the room is not air-conditioned, open the window for airing while you work (but only as far as comfortable if cold or stormy). Empty ashtrays into tin box in supply basket, wash and dry them, empty waste basket, wipe out and return to proper place, use sweeper if needed before turning down beds.

To Remove Spreads

1. Fold neatly from head to foot.
2. Fold again parallel with head and foot.
3. Fold from edge to middle of bed, overlapping center about one-third.
4. Fold remaining edge over this and fold again to size that will fit in drawer.
5. Remove extra blanket from bottom drawer and put spread in its place.

To Place Extra Blanket on Bed

1. Put it across foot of bed with bindings parallel to foot.
2. Unfold from center.
3. Tuck one edge under at foot of bed.
4. Pull top edge about one-third of way to top of bed leaving extra length in two wide folds, with bound edge at top so it can be pulled up easily if desired.

If only one bed is to be used, turn down the one nearest the bath and place slippers at that side. Where two people are registered, turn the beds down toward each other and put slippers between. Turn bedclothes down the width that top sheet is turned over blankets, then fold diagonally from outer edge of top to center of bed so that one-half of top edge is parallel with side of bed.

In the bathroom, wash and dry soiled glasses, using glass towel only, wash and dry basin and tub, if used, and exchange soiled towels and face cloths for clean. Leave soap unless too small for use and exchange floor or tub mats only if wet or soiled. Wipe any wet spots from floor and flush toilet to check. Close window, adjust blind or shade and draperies, put out all lights except one on night stand, close and lock door. Do not forget to report anything out of order, such as dripping faucet, burned-out light bulb, etc.

Procedures for Other Employees

Lavatory Attendants—Men and Women

Outsiders often judge an institution by the way you work. In Hospitals, Clubs, Colleges, and Schools, visitors are usually in only one other part of the building, while in Hotels and Motels they may patronize only the restaurant, cocktail lounge or bar. In either case they are apt to use the lavatory and the impression of cleanliness or the lack of it is made largely by how thoroughly you have done your work. We depend on your pride in the establishment and your faithfulness in following the work schedule to prevent complaints.

Day Service

Clean these places in the order of their opening, with Coffee Shop first. Check on the others to see if anything was neglected by night workers. If so, notify the first assistant so that a report can be made to the supervisor of night cleaning. After this, attend to employees' toilets. A trip to the Coffee Shop before 11:30 is necessary and to all rooms serving lunch both during and after the meal. A thorough cleaning is needed afterward. Your schedule shows other visits required to all places.

Night Service

Follow the routine of rounds your schedule calls for and if any special room is crowded, check more often. Do not forget to clean the employees' toilets thoroughly after closing of Coffee Shop at 10 P.M.

Parlor Maid—Day

At the times assigned, take care of all ladies' lounges and lavatories to keep both furniture and floors dusted, waste baskets emptied, and chairs in place. On each round, wash and wipe basins, check on soap, exchange soiled for clean towels or replenish stock of paper ones, clean toilet bowls, empty trash cans, and be sure toilet paper receptacles are full. Do not forget to report needed repairs or unusual occurrences.

Parlor Maid—Night

Starting with cocktail room, follow routine on day work schedule, making rounds at least once an hour. If a guest is ill, notify assistant manager and linen room at once. Fit in at least two trips to employees' toilets before midnight. If guests request safety pins, needle and thread, etc., be prepared and give them pleasantly.

PROCEDURES FOR REPORTING EMPLOYEE ACCIDENTS

This is the notice sent by Management in one large hotel.

To All Department Heads:

There is a nurse on duty in the First Aid Room on the 16th floor from 10 A.M. to 5 P.M. daily except Saturdays, Sundays and holidays.

It is important for you to send all employees who are injured in the hotel to the nurse at once, no matter how small the injury may seem.

For a minor accident occurring while the nurse is off duty, first aid should be given at the place assigned to your department for this treatment. These places are:

Assistant manager's office—for front office and lobby floor employees.
Banquet department—15th or 16th floor, for those employees only.
Engineering department—in basement, for them and laundry employees.
Kitchen—at food checker's desk, for all kitchen workers and waiters.
Linen room—for the housekeeping staff and all other workers on that floor.

Timekeeper—for street floor workers and any street floor restaurant help.

These stations are checked for equipment the first of every month by the nurse, but if extra supplies are needed between times, do not hesitate to ask for them. A written requisition from the department head is required.

In case of a serious accident, call the assistant manager on duty, who will arrange for a cab to doctor's office or hospital.

Any accident when the nurse is not in the house must be reported in writing and put under the door of her office, so that she may fill out the report for the insurance company immediately. The report to her must include time, place, cause and type of accident, the person's name, address, and timecard number. Report is signed by department head and taken in duplicate to the manager. She retains one copy in her files.

Because I believe these rules are important to both the welfare of employees and the hotel, I expect your hearty co-operation.

Signed _____, Manager

CHAPTER 11

Job Evaluation

This is the process of deciding the value of one job in comparison to others so as to establish fair wages for the quantity and quality of work it requires. It can decrease employee grievances growing out of wage inequalities, stimulate the slow or poor workers to improve the quality of their work, and remove uncertainty as to promotion and pay increases. It enables management to develop a justifiable wage policy for use in collective bargaining and furnishes a systematic method of wage cost control.

Essential Factors

The factors to be considered vary somewhat but these seem to cover the fundamentals. They are the ones outlined by Faye H. Javens, Job Analyst–Hospital Service Association of Pittsburgh. For some positions, education, training and experience would equal in value all the others combined. It must be realized that proper differentials in wages must be maintained between supervisor and staff.

1. Knowledge—Formal or informal education necessary to do the job satisfactorily.
2. Experience and training—Past and amount needed to acquire necessary skill.
3. Skill, dexterity and accuracy—manual and mental—Speed of coordination, precision in application of mental and manual skill.
4. Responsibility—for self only, supervision, safety of others, materials, equipment.
5. Physical effort—Muscular exertion and time it is used.
6. Mental effort—Extent of application of mental skill.
7. Working conditions:
   a. Hazards—possibility of personal injury.

    b. Surroundings—working conditions, climatic, etc.

    c. Connected expense—tools, replacement only.

8. Fatigue—Due to mental or physical effort or disagreeable surroundings.

9. Functional duties—Those required in correlating work of job into unified program.

Performance evaluation is quite as important and includes the following factors:

1. Quality of work.
2. Quantity of work.
3. Job knowledge.
4. Dependability.
5. Initiative.
6. Cooperation.
7. Ability and willingness to learn.
8. Personality.
9. Personal appearance.
10. Judgment.
11. Percent of time given to each kind of work, mental, physical, etc., should be considered in assigning value.

Naturally, separate plans must be made for skilled workers, for supervisors and for top executives. This task demands the best thinking of both management and department heads. For more complete treatment of the subject, I refer you to Professor Donald E. Lundberg's excellent book, *Personnel Management in Hotels and Restaurants,* in which there are graphs and full explanations.

Employee's Report Card

As a rule, two sets of records are examined when considering an employee's promotion, transfer, or dismissal. One is the card on which is recorded the complete report of complaints against the employee and the action taken about it. For this, the department head gets the worker's version of the incident, explains what was wrong and what should have been done. The matter is discussed (without use of names) at the next staff meeting to help other employees. The card notation includes the complaint, what caused the trouble, and what steps were taken to prevent its recurrence. Copies of this are sent to the executive office and manager, and one kept by the department head.

A form for this card follows:

Employee's Demerit Notice

Name _____ Department _____ Date _____
Explanation of Complaint _____
_____
_____

Reasons Given by Employee _____
_____

Warning or Penalty _____
_____

Department Head's Signature   Employee's Signature

When a guest compliments an employee for courtesy, quality of service, or good work, or if the supervisor commends him or her for something, this is recorded as follows: (Copies also sent to executive office, manager and department head.)

Employee's Merit Notice

Name _____ Department _____ Date _____
Wording of Compliment _____
_____
_____

Department Head's Signature   Employee's Signature

These reports are valuable since they give the following results:

1. Shows whether further training is needed.
2. Assists in selection for promotion.
3. Assists in deciding on transfers to other departments.
4. Makes supervisors more aware of employees' qualities, good and bad.

5. Determines salary.
6. Encourages greater effort.
7. Informs employee of supervisor's opinion of his work.

Merit Rating

This is often called Service Rating. It is the appraisal of an individual worker in meeting the requirements of the job. It measures the employee's effectiveness in his present position and his qualifications for advancement. It is used by the United States Government, many State Government departments, and often by industry of all kinds, colleges, hospitals, and increasingly, by hotels.

The survey necessary to set up such a system is less expensive if one of the company personnel can be trained to make it, as he or she is better qualified to choose the type of system best suited to the institution because of familiarity with the operation and because they must help carry out the project.

Any Merit Rating system must consider the following characteristics:

1. Appearance—Neat and clean.
2. Disposition—Pleasant and cheerful.
3. Physical fitness—Good eyesight and hearing, good feet and back, stamina.
4. Personality traits—Pleasing, agreeable voice—not too high pitched—good manners, quiet worker.
5. Mental ability—Responsive, not too slow in understanding orders.
6. Working habits—Thorough, dependable, steady.
7. Attitudes—To supervisors, obedient—to fellow employees, cooperative—to guests, helpful.

Ratings:

Outstanding: 90 to 100%
Excellent: 80 to 90%
Fair to Good: 70 to 80%
Poor or Weak: 60 to 70%
Unsatisfactory: below 60%

The Connecticut Service Rating Institution warns, "Make sure that:

1. "You have not been influenced by personal considerations such as friendship or prejudice.
2. "The rating reflects the actual performance of the employee over the whole rating period and is not based on isolated instances of success or failure.
3. "You have not considered length of service which will be credited as a separate item by the personnel director."

Records of employees should show qualifications for advancement in the same departments, or jobs in other departments.

The poor worker deserves to be informed as to where he or she has failed. This may lead to increased interest in the job and in greater effort to do it as well as required, even if those results are not immediately evident.

Ratings must be scored by two or three people if the analysis is to be impersonal. It is useful in developing better employees by showing them where they need to improve and by removing the uncertainty of advancement. It also helps them realize some of the qualities, besides good work, which are essential for promotion.

Some places give prizes to those showing the greatest improvement in a stated time. Others present a monthly award for the highest rating in efficiency, courtesy and neatness, with winners competing for the annual award. Any method is good which increases the skill of the individual and the teamwork of the staff. Industry has led the way in recognizing the importance of education for all employees and often their prize is a course of study of interest to the winner or that will be of value in advancement. This is an area where hotels are far behind other similar organizations. Hospitals aid ambitious workers by paying all or part of the fees for approved courses and motels encourage continuing education to a far greater extent than hotels. May not this be one factor in the dearth of available applicants for top positions?

Time and Motion Study and Work Simplification

This means the study of present work procedures in an effort to find better, easier, and less time-consuming ways to do the work. It includes eliminating unnecessary motions, simplifying tools, using up-to-date equipment and techniques, thus saving time. It aims to plan schedules and systems to produce the best possible results not only in less time but with less fatigue to the worker, in an attempt to increase efficiency and thus curb the ever increasing labor cost by better performance of assigned duties.

Time Study comes first for we must know how long a process takes *now*, before we see if it is really shortened by any routine we may try. One of the first time studies of hotel operations was made by students from Purdue University in 1948, it analyzed the customary method of getting a "checkout" ready for occupancy at the Sherman Hotel in Chicago. The group worked on the elimination of labor and time saving and proved it possible to reduce both time required and worker's fatigue. One way, in use for some time at the Brown Palace Hotel in Denver, is the "One Trip Around" bed making system, as described in Chapter 10. Research is finding many ways to improve the labor saving advantages of all sorts of equipment, kinds of cleaners, and methods for their use. The housekeeping executive is expected to keep up with these advances and use them to reduce costs.

Housekeeping workers are no different from other people in not wanting to change their ways, so they must be sold on the new techniques or products by proving them to be easier, leaving the workers less tired at night. Training newcomers in the new ways often helps in retraining the oldtimers when they see how these people like the new methods.

Work simplification often means greater guest satisfaction and decreased costs due to using the time saved for better daily cleaning. This saves on heavy work of carpet washing, polishing, upholstery cleaning and the like, so reducing the work done by men at higher pay. Intelligent study of this always results in a lessened work load of some sort. In older houses it may mean the removal of seldom-used pieces of furniture—perhaps a dressing table or chiffonier—with the resulting saving of dusting, polishing, and moving for vacuuming. Today's new hotels and motels are fortunate for they are most often furnished with "built-ins," where only one side of the piece needs dusting or with multi-purpose pieces like the dresser, desk, baggage rack and even television combination. Add to this reduced labor and time saving decoration, the fact that all furniture is liquor and stain proof and fire resistant and it is easy to see what a reduction there is in the labor cost. Often equipment can help in work simplification if new and more effective models are bought. Since these are likely to be lighter in weight, the fatigue element is reduced also.

Since our aim is courteous, efficient, contented employees, it is our obligation to train them in the best methods of room care. This means careful analysis of present procedures, efforts to lessen the time and motion used and supplementing our own ideas for this improvement by adapting the techniques of others to our special conditions.

Naturally there will never come a time when the entire staff is 100% productive but they will increase in efficiency and work will be of better quality as working conditions improve and they are less tired toward the close of the day.

The Exit Interview

This also requires an impersonal attitude, so is often assigned to a member of the personnel department for discovering the *real* reason for leaving. In the case of good workers, the housekeeper will want to talk to them to see if it is possible to change their minds or if not, to promote a pleasant feeling toward the organization, where it is actually a better chance, illness, or moving out of the neighborhood. This leaves the door open for a return if the place does not prove better or if circumstances change. This is good public relations.

Usually a printed form is used which has questions designed to reveal faults in working conditions, employee relations, methods, equipment or other conditions. If leaving a department which has a large turnover, the individual's answers may show why. Is there something wrong with any of the above mentioned things or are current hours or rates of pay out of line with similar jobs in the area? An explanation of the "better job" may show faults of which the department is not conscious. If the employee is actually a misfit, may

CHAPTER 12

Personnel Relations

It has been said that just as governments are people, so also are institutions, for the image of both is the picture painted by the citizens of the former and the employees of the latter. Mr. Zaffy of Sheraton Corporation of America, describes it as "The composite personality of all its workers, the catalytic agent which produces the high morale and team work that make things go." This is why so much emphasis is placed on *good* employee relations these days.

It is true that fundamental employee relation policies are decided by top management, influenced by many factors—traditions, social approval of the community—attitude of labor and actions of competitors, among others. These policies must be firmly established, yet flexible enough to meet new conditions. They should be simple and easily understood. The responsibility for seeing that these ideas are carried out is actually that of department heads and the importance of this part of the executive housekeeper's duty cannot be overstressed. The ideal of a courteous, well groomed, carefully trained, efficient staff with the high morale necessary for smooth functioning requires that good personnel relations begin with the first interviews, increase during orientation and training and develop unceasingly throughout the entire term of employment.

Every Housekeeping Employee a Salesman

All employees of this department come in direct contact with patrons and must be made to realize their value as salesmen for the establishment. They need to understand that "The Guest Comes First" as the most important person in the place because the higher the house count, the more sure they are of their jobs since it is the room rent which meets the payroll. They must recognize that their quiet efficiency, courteous willing service and pleasant manners will impress the guest with the desirability of a long stay, of another visit when possible, and a recommendation to friends as a good place to stay. The lack of any of these qualities decreases that good impression.

Only those who are proud of the institution, of their part in its upkeep, and are happily adjusted, can sell guests on the fact that it is a good place to stay. The basic needs of individuals must be met before their work can satisfy them, meet the requirements of management and please the guests. Since the attitude of the department head is reflected all the way down the line, the satisfactory worker indicates capable, considerate guidance and effective housekeeping management. Labor turnover is largely due to lack of one or more of these things.

The following conditions are desired by all workers.

1. *Suitable work*—that for which one is fitted, therefore enjoys. This is recognized as important and since all institutions need a variety of services, employees are selected to fit the one for which they feel competent and which makes them happy.

2. *Steady work*—this is not easy where payroll must be governed by occupancy. It may be best to hire a minimum full-time staff with relief and part-time workers on call for peak periods.

3. *Comfortable working conditions*—good personal facilities— clean comfortable rest, lunch, and locker rooms, good food, smart, well fitted uniforms, up-to-date equipment, and the right cleaners for various surfaces, with adequate linen and guest supplies to prevent needless return trips to rooms.

4. *Effective "on the job" training* is a *must* and is covered in detail in Chapter 8.

5. *Pleasant working companions*—governed by careful selection, eliminating troublemakers, and by the development of good morale and team work.

6. *Good supervision*—choosing a supervisor is *so* important for she is expected to keep work up to standard at all times. Strict but kind oversight is needed to be sure that Mary tidied her hair after shutting the window; that John vacuumed the bath ventilator, and that Susie dusted the light bulb and straightened the shade, with its seam toward the wall. She must praise

Kate for learning how to make a good bed, and Jim for the shining brass sand jars. Each worker is different, so she must learn their strength and weakness and treat them accordingly. The inspectress is a *very* important person.

7. *Good pay*—as compared with other industries is not easy when the labor market is tight, so extra attention must be paid to other conditions—fringe benefits, and the best possible working conditions. With some workers their skills are in demand only seasonally, so steadier work is an asset.

8. *Opportunities for expressing their ideas* for improving their jobs. Often time or labor saving plans of real merit advanced by workers are adopted by Management. Personal credit and awards are greatly valued, but in case an idea is not suitable, there should be an explanation as to why it cannot be used. Failure in this often discourages further efforts.

9. *Chance for advancement*—is a big help in keeping desirable people. The policy of having two people in training for every supervisory position is of help. Naturally the ones chosen must have the qualities or potentialities necessary for the position and be willing to train for it. In some places the line up is definitely outlined so anyone can see where the present job leads. This is good.

10. *Suitable hours* are possible because of the 24 hour day requirements, so people can be fitted into the time best suited to their needs.

Morale Builders

Several of these have been mentioned in previous chapters but one of the most encouraging at present is the added respect being shown for housekeeping employees. Upgrading in the hospitality business includes not only renovations and redecoration but the equally, if not more important, revised picture of the workers who care for them. At Chalfonte-Haddon Hall, a card in each guest room states "Mrs. _____ is responsible for the care of your room. Please let her know if there is any way in which she can make you more comfortable." At the Brown Palace Hotel in

Denver, the maids are called "Floor Housekeepers," their immediate supervisors are "Inspectresses." Mrs. Soper the housekeeper is "Director of Housekeeping and Maintenance." Many housemen are now called "Maintenance Men" or "Sanitors." This is a big boost to morale for it denotes and encourages increased respect for the work and worker. All employees must be made to realize their importance as part of the working team, the real contribution their good work makes to the success of the establishment.

Now that we have so many more guests from foreign countries, it is standard practice to discover in the first interview if the applicant speaks another language, which one, from what part of the country he or she comes and their education. If hired, this is a part of the record and is kept on file in both Department and Front office files so it will be available in case it is needed by a visitor from another country. If such service is offered it impresses the guest with the consideration for his comfort and adds to the employees' prestige among his fellow workers. Whenever a member of the staff can be used for additional work in which he or she has talent or experience, it gives a boost to morale and also helps in many emergencies. If the record card shows experience in office work, sewing, baby sitting, or any other specialty it should be used when possible to increase self confidence and awareness of the value of experience. It also increases their appreciation of the establishment as a good place to work, one ingredient of the greatly valued good morale.

Impartial enforcement of rules is important, for the need to be treated honestly, fairly and considerately is a basic need of every individual. They also want to know that the housekeeper and all supervisory assistants have their interests at heart. A pleasant morning greeting, asking if yesterday's headache has gone, if baby or husband is better, mother back from the hospital or newly married children heard from—anything showing *real* understanding and interest in personal problems—all are morale builders. Pretense is quickly recognized and resented. To pass on praise from guest or Management in a staff meeting helps them realize that their good work is important to the success of the establishment—that they are vital parts of the business. If a guest complains of service or manner, get the worker's story before criticizing. You may find the intention right, but judgment wrong. By acknowledging the first, your explanation of how to meet a similar situation will be more effective.

All employees want to know what is going on within the organization—plans for new construction, redecoration, the possibility of changing management or ownership, so when they are asked about it they can say, "Yes, the Boss told us about it." This increases their prestige with friends by indicating they are a part of those "in the know." What an employee does not know *can* hurt his pride.

It is always wise to find out what makes a worker unhappy and to try to rectify it, for all turnover is both expensive and time consuming, to be avoided whenever possible. If not able to change the condition it may be wise to let the person go, rather than have the attitude spread. The Exit Interview, mentioned in Chapter 11 may show the cause of the discontent more clearly.

We have been speaking so far of our responsibilities to employees. What of theirs toward us? Is it not possible that at least part of Union difficulties may be due to a lack of stressing this at the bargaining session? A realistic consideration of conditions must reveal that there can be no increased earnings for the workers unless there are many guests and the number of these depends on their satisfaction with the service. Only when employees are doing their best work, can this be done, so it seems logical to ask of them a good day's work, loyalty to their employers, and the required attitudes toward guests. If these are not achieved, it results in lessened housecount, fewer, less effective workers, and further loss of business. In many industries the necessity for really co-operative relations between Management and Labor is acknowledged and negotiations conducted from this point of view. When this becomes customary in our business, we may expect decreased friction and increased efficiency.

Part III

ORGANIZATION AND MANAGEMENT

CHAPTER **13**

The Linen Room

According to their functions, linen rooms vary greatly in size, shape, and location; the latter because they were sometimes forgotten on the architect's plan, so had to be tucked into any corner available. Some are on the roof, others in the basement, or anywhere in between. Today's institutional architects realize the importance of this housekeeping service station, so in consultation with manager and department head, choose the proper location. It may be on an office floor, in an unsaleable spot or next to the executive housekeeper's office. In large buildings it is as near as possible to the service elevator in order to save time for the staff and linen delivery. It should be near an outside door in motels and small hotels for the same reasons.

The most nearly ideal service floor arrangement I have seen is one where store rooms for blankets, general supplies, and linen reserve; drapery, slipcover, and upholstery wokshops; also those for refinishing furniture and linen distribution were on the same floor as the linen room. This enabled the first assistant to supervise the shop work as she went back and forth through the corridor, so there was little chance for wasted time.

Size and Lighting

A 12 x 15 foot square room, if well planned, is adequate for the small house, where one attendant also acts as seamstress. A larger room is needed for the large establishment having several seamstresses as well as an attendant. In both cases, effective service demands careful attention to good ventilation and lighting. If there is an outside window, the sewing machines should be placed so the seamstresses sit with the light at their left. Where there is glaring sunlight, it is wise to furnish a screen for the lower half of each window (which can be pushed up on dark days). The screen which deflects direct rays of the sun are worth the cost because of lessened eyestrain and consequent headaches. Side lights may be needed for dark days or night work. Each seamstress needs a shelf at the left of the machine for articles to be made or mended, a linen truck in front of it, into which finished work can be dropped to go to the laundry for pressing. She also needs a table or shelf at the right for blankets or other things which do not need laundry attention. The choice of wall paint will determine, to a large extent, the amount of ceiling light needed. Where there is plenty of outside light, a soft tint of any color can be used. Otherwise white may be preferable. The electric company will gladly advise on the correct type of wattage necessary. Local fire laws usually require a sprinkler system and strictly enforced rules against smoking in this room.

Planning

Each linen room must be planned according to its particular functions, so before going into explicit recommendations, let us see what some of these functions may be. In all types of institutions, the linen room is the heart of the Housekeeping Department, the center of effective operation. It is a *storage place* for the many things required by employees in carrying on their duties and usually for bed and bath linen and table napery. It is a *distribution center* for linens; a *production center*, where various articles are made or mended; and, most important, the *information center* for guests, managers, other department heads, and employees.

As a storage place, it must be conveniently arranged to save time and steps. The door and aisles must be wide enough to allow a truck to deliver or pick up supplies and linen directly to and from shelves. Across the door, a drop shelf is handy as a counter for receiving or passing out various things and it also keeps out those who do not belong in the room. A key rack behind the open door is a safe and convenient place to keep maid's pass keys so they can be given out or replaced without extra steps. Things most often called for should be kept nearest the door, with bulky or heavy articles on the bottom shelves to avoid strain, and the lighter ones above. Table linens are usually sent for only twice a day and can be further from the door as busboys go direct to shelves with a truck to get them, under the attendant's supervision.

The width, depth, and space between shelves is determined by the size of folded articles for which they are used. Whether flat or contour sheets, plain or boxed daybed covers, cotton, silk, chenille or other spreads are standard, all govern the measurements of shelves. The standard stock for rooms and table linen in circulation decides the amount of shelving needed. There must be room for the emergency stock for use in peak periods on top shelves carefully covered (possibly by discarded spreads) to prevent soiling or mussing. A bulletin board for notices and posters should be placed outside in the corridor. A blackboard for listing checkouts, a wall clock, and a hook for banquet department requisitions are useful.

Every linen room needs a center table for sorting, laying out uniforms and supplies and on which work may be cut out for the seamstress. One that is 48 inches long, 36 inches wide, and 36 inches or more high, according to the height of the attendant is satisfactory. Such a table should also allow for three 16-inch deep drawers on each side for uniforms, etc. with toe room left under the table.

A narrow drop-leaf table or shelf is a great help at times when something goes wrong in the laundry and bath towels need folding, for instance. The day's supply of matches can be protected in a small tin bread box. The attendant's desk or table is most convenient when placed near telautograph or other means of communication between departments. In addition to the phone, she has the book recording all calls, deliveries of items or those received from checkouts or other departments, with outgoing and incoming spindles for orders. A hand truck for bringing up things from the receiving department is needed. First Aid is kept here for use of employees of this department.

In motels and small hotels, the housekeeper's office is a corner, partitioned off from the linen room for privacy in interviewing applicants, dealing with employees and conferences with other people. It needs only a desk, files and two chairs, so does not take much space. In larger houses, it may be an office on the floor with others or one near the linen room. Usually it has an adjoining office for secretary and first assistant.

Linen Circulation

Most small operations find an even exchange of linen—clean for soiled—the best way to keep control, but in the larger institutions this is not practical. Consequently the distribution of clean bed and bath linen is handled differently. If it is sent from laundry to linen room for storage, it is distributed from there by a houseman to the floor closets and soiled sent to laundry by chute or in large bags marked with floor and section. Hospitals and many other places have found it a time-and-labor-saver to send this directly from laundry to floor in open shelved carts similar to those used for sending food from one place to another. These are left in closets from which shelves are removed and when empty, are wheeled back to the laundry for a refill. This system is being used more all the time, to save the extra handling and so reduce the payroll. A great many places have been using the laundry as the storage center for table linen and find an even exchange system works out by this method. Sometimes the linen room continues to take care of mending table napery and make-overs but if the size of the establishment calls for an extra worker for this, that person often works in the laundry.

Linen Room Attendant

If there are more than 100 rooms, a full time linen room attendant is necessary, during the day at least. She is the "room clerk" of this department for it is her voice that is heard and her attitude sensed by guests calling about any kind of housekeeping service. If she seems disinterested, careless about filling an order, or is discourteous in any way, it reflects on the whole organization. The wrong person in this position offends patrons and department heads, and lowers staff morale almost before it is realized.

The special qualities required for this position are not easy to find fully developed, so there must be great care in selection and thorough orientation as to the work of all departments and staff members. The training must be very thorough also. Besides a pleasing voice and manner, she needs a very even disposition, the ability to switch her attention quickly from one thing to another without getting nervous or confused, and good common sense. She must learn where to use her own judgment and when it is necessary to refer the matter to housekeeper or manager. Her attitude toward employees must always be courteous and helpful. Accuracy is most important in recording orders, the time taken, name of worker, and when completed. If you have someone satisfactory in this position, you are fortunate. Be grateful and let her know how much you appreciate her. As we have mentioned, have one of the other workers, who shows traits necessary for this job, in training for relief and vacations.

The Attendant's Duties

It is customary for this employee to open the linen room about one-half hour before the others come on duty, so as to have uniforms, aprons, dusters and other supplies ready to give them with the keys. She goes off duty one-half hour earlier than the others, so the one in training or an inspectress takes over after she tells of anything special to be taken care of. Both of them must be careful to leave messages for the incoming night woman so there will be no slip-up of any kind. According to the size of the house, the attendant may distribute linen or only relieve the one who does; may supervise the seamstresses; or a seamstress may be in charge.

The checkouts from the room clerk are relayed to the floors by the attendant and the okayed reports made by an inspectress after they were given to the room clerk are erased from the board. Space does not permit full details of this person's probable duties, for they vary greatly in different institutions.

CHAPTER 14

Controls

Rigid is the word for the kind of control necessary for governing the purchases and the economical use and replacement of all the different items used in this department, for every one of which the housekeeper is accountable. These include linen of all kinds, furniture, floor coverings, draperies, curtains, accessories, guest supplies, cleaning materials and equipment, uniforms, and whatever you can name that is used in this division of institutional operation.

Control begins with the decision as to the amount of each item needed, which differs with the size, type, and policies of the house. Furniture, par for instance, depends on the number of rooms, while bed and bath linen requirements are figured by the number and kind of beds. Certain equipment must be bought according to the number of employees, while the amount of furniture polish needed is determined by the number and kinds of pieces in use and their finish. This means separate standards for par stock of the various categories.

After this list of requirements is made for each item, comes the decision of specifications; then price comparison for the same quality and delivery service, before buying; careful checking of invoice and bill; then suitable storage and distribution methods are adopted; training in the proper care of all working equipment; and the use and proportion of cleaning powders or liquids as approved by the manufacturers. All of these are phases of control, as is the decision as to when each thing has passed its usefulness and must be discarded. If one of these steps is neglected, the full value of any item is not obtained.

We have sometimes thought of linen control as the only one for which the housekeeper is answerable and this, largely in relation to losses. It is very important, but only a part of her control duty, as we have seen. There are at least four people interested in this subject and each has a different definition for it.

"Enough linen in circulation and emergency reserve to keep the work running smoothly," says the executive housekeeper.

"Accurate records of linen in circulation and storage" is the accountant's definition.

The purchasing department claims it is "Balanced buying which permits gradual replacement."

To management, it means "Efficient managing so that what we need is on hand when we need it."

These differing points of view are all true.

Only the executive housekeeper has the key to the reserve linen storeroom, so full responsibility is her's for accuracy of count. Thus, the receipt of incoming linen and its issue must be under her direct supervision. There are different methods of keeping track of receiving and issue. One is a book of records for each, differing in color. The records are made in duplicate, with the original from each sent to the accounting department. The auditor usually checks the quarterly, or semi-annual count with the first assistant or may do it with a member of his staff. These inventories show the number of each item on hand at the last count, with what has been issued and received since then—thus showing any shortage or overage.

The reserve storeroom should be large enough to keep room and table linens entirely separate. When receipts have included odd amounts (one-fourth or one-half dozen), these are best issued first to make the count easier by having only packages of the same size. A large open stack of shelves in the center of the room is good for storing large or bulky things and makes it easy to count from both sides. Mr. L. A. Bradley, Laundry Consultant for the American Hotel Association advises that *cotton* things should not be stored for any length of time before washing to remove starch and finishing chemicals. These chemicals have a tendency to attract insects, to become dry and brittle, and sometimes turn pink. They should be rewrapped as a protection from dust and light. He says that *linen* may be stored for a long time *if* wrapped in dark paper to keep free from dust and color change. A well ventilated, not too dry, cool, dark place is best.

Control of linen is easier in small houses, where a "clean for soiled" exchange is the rule, so there is small chance for loss expect from souvenir-hunting guests. Better control methods for the larger operations are always being sought.

Inventory

A complete inventory of all linen in reserve and circulation is generally considered necessary as a means of keeping these up to par by replacing the losses indicated in the latter and the amount therefore issued from the former. It is usually taken bi-monthly, quarterly, or sometimes only semi-annually. A few chains consider the cost of labor greater than results merit. This expense is avoided when linen is rented. Because of this and also because rental does not tie up money in reserve stock or add to maintenance expense for mending or laundry, its use is increasing and rental cost is decreasing. Many motels and small hotels find it less expensive than owning their own linen.

An inventory needs the cooperation of all department heads using linen, so they must be informed as to time of day and proper procedures at least the day before one is to be taken. Here is a sample of such notification:

NOTICE OF INVENTORY DAY

Notice to Manager of
    _____ Coffee Shop
    _____ Cocktail Lounge
    _____ Main Dining Room
    _____ Men's Bar
Linen inventory will be taken tomorrow _____ at 3 P.M.
                                        DATE

Tonight when your room closes please send all *clean* linen (not in use) to the linen room. Soiled linen is to go to laundry at 3 P.M. tomorrow and all clean linen left in supply closet, at the bar or on tables, counted. Please use following form and send count to linen room by 4 P.M. Thank you.

Executive Housekeeper

Procedure for Linen Count in Food Department

The first assistant (or housekeeper, in small houses) takes the count in any rooms where there is no employee available at the time designated, possibly in banquet or private dining rooms.

Both room and food department linen counts are started at the same time. No linen given out preceding this time is counted in the linen room and nothing distributed afterward is counted elsewhere. For example, if 50 tablecloths and 100 napkins are given out from the linen room for the main dining room before noon, they were not counted because the soiled ones taken to laundry are counted there and the clean ones left, go into dining room count. This count is kept separate from that of room linens, even to pieces needing mending as well as discards.

Form for Food Inventory

Date				Room			
Napkins	White	Colored	Cloths	White	Colored	Tray Cloths	Side Towels
Tea 18 x 18 22 x 22			45 x 45 54 x 54 72 x 72 72 x 90 90 x 90				

Procedure for Rooms Count—Day Maids

When the maids are trained to take the count, following is one method:

1. Remove all soiled linen from beds and bath.
2. Make up the rooms and count all clean linens on beds and in baths.
3. Include blankets on beds and in dresser drawers. Do not overlook anything in dresser drawers or on closet shelves in occupied rooms.

4. At 3 P.M. the laundry chute is closed in order for laundry to start count. Maids take from floor closets to their carts the linen needed for making up the last rooms. After this linen has been removed, the inspectresses count the linen in closets on the floors she supervises.

5. At 3:50 the chute is opened *at the top* for soiled linen picked up after 3:00 P.M. and kept open over night. It is removed for counting before the maids come in the next morning.

6. Maids list numbers of any rooms they cannot get into to make up and turn these numbers in at the linen room on their way out for the night maids to count.

Procedure for Rooms Count—Night Maids

1. Night maids count linen only in rooms on day maids' list given them.

2. They count only *clean* linen found in room, because the soiled will be counted in laundry and the clean they bring has been counted by the inspectress.

3. These room numbers are turned in to linen room on the way home.

Date_____ INVENTORY OF LINEN IN ROOMS Taken by_____
Section

Room Number	Spring Covers		Bed Pads		Sheets		Pillow Cases		Blankets	Blanket Covers		Spreads		Face Towels	Bath Towels	Hand Towels	Wash Cloths	Bath Mats	Bath Rugs	Shower Curtains
	L	S	L	S	L	S	L	S	L	S	L	S	L	S							

From the lists of all maids, inspectresses, seamstress (showing discards and those in mending pile), laundry, and linen room attendants, the above inventory form is compiled—after the addition of results of reserve stock count, and the number of items in the "stolen" report book kept by the first assistant as illustrated.

ARTICLES REPORTED MISSING FROM ROOMS DURING JULY, 195_

Date	Room	By Whom	Towels Bath.Face	Bath Rug.Mat	Floor Rug	Pillows	Blankets	Other Articles
1	210	J.Price Vac. Man						Picture
5	340	S.Reid Maid	1					
7	509	J.Jones Maid	2					
10	550	Mrs.Pry Ass't Hkp		1			1	

Each institution has its own forms for linen in circulation in rooms, and food service, and in reserve for each. If it is customary to make over discards, there should be an added column for "Conversions" or "Makeovers" before the "Total Count." From this inventory, a shortened form is made for the manager and/or auditor.

INVENTORY OF LINEN IN CIRCULATION FOR MANAGER OR ACCOUNTING DEPARTMENT

Items	Last Count	Add. Put in Circ.	Total	Discards and Known Losses	Total Should be	Actual Count	Under	Over
Bed Pads								
Sheets Large								
Sheets Small								

When there is a great discrepancy, a recount of that item is taken and if not much pick-up is made there must be a thorough investigation as to a possible cause of the loss. Sometimes the laundry has thrown out soiled or torn pieces. There should be a very strict rule that *nothing* should be discarded anywhere except in the linen room. Occasionally a thief is discovered. So far there is no *perfect* control method. The surest is the "clean for soiled" exchange. Following are some ideas which may help prolong the use of linens:

1. Identify by marking or name weaving.
2. Use even exchange when possible.
3. Keep all linen supply closets locked, using a spring lock.
4. Keep maid's linen cart halfway across the open door when working in a room, so no one will be tempted to take anything off the cart.
5. Adapt to your own circumstances the ideas you may find in all sorts of places, especially the manuals published by Hotel and Hospital Associations.

CAUSES OF SHORT LIFE FOR LINENS

Both rooms and dining room linen are so expensive that linen conservation is very important, so let us look at some ways in which it is thoughtlessly ruined:

1. Improper use of a napkin to wipe a metal or for cleaning shoes.
2. Poor care by putting damp uniforms, table or bed linens in laundry hamper, thus courting mildew.
3. Carelessness in storing and carrying clean linens so they get mussed before using makes extra laundering necessary.
4. Putting stained pieces in with damp linen so that stain spreads, especially when the soiled linen is not sent to laundry quickly.
5. Failure to rotate linen so that same wears too quickly and other pieces get soiled on the folds and have to be washed too often for number of times used.
6. Unnecessary use of bleach because of neglect to wash hands before using towels.
7. Scattering soiled table linen on kitchen floor instead of using drop box at door.
8. Stock in circulation too small, so life of linen shortened by too frequent washing.
9. Sometimes an incorrect laundry formula will weaken the fibers.

10. Use of medicines, creams, lotions or hair oil, all hard to remove from bed clothes.

11. Carelessness in stripping the bed, straining fibers.

Ways of impressing employees with the money value of linen losses are always being looked for by management. One that made a real impression was the comparison of the cost of different articles with the hourly pay of those who use them.

CHAPTER 15

Budgets

An annual budget is required of most executive housekeepers these days. It is often the largest one in number of people and products included, although the chief engineer's may be somewhat more costly. It is a time-consuming project and demands, where possible, complete and accurate records of the previous year's experience. Where this is not available, or for the opening of a new place, it is necessary to make an estimate which may err in the calculation of one or many things. Naturally the only realistic budget is made from exact accounting records of *all* annual expenses—payroll, equipment, cleaning materials, guest supplies, repairs (on all sorts of things), replacements, etc., and also management's definite schedule of planned renovation and redecoration. At times these last two are budgeted separately and the payroll may be on a separate form. However these are included in the final form submitted to manager and/or treasurer.

Since the budget is an estimate of the department's cost for the coming year, it must include pending payroll decreases (by reassignment of jobs, so as to do the same work with fewer people or temporary closing of a section); increases due to management policies, government or union rulings, or additions to the property; purchase of everything included in plans for changes and replacements—carpets or other floor coverings, furniture, upholstery materials, draperies, glass curtains, window shades or blinds, lamps, accessories etc.; cleaning materials and equipment; uniforms and guest room supplies, plus the cost of contract work.

The estimated cost of all these items must be at the highest price paid, since even when buying in quantity and discounting all bills, there is little hope for lower than last year's prices. Do not forget to include the repairs made on various things and their upkeep—piano tuning, for instance.

The request for replacement by new equipment, or anything more expensive must be accompanied by the explanation of *why* it is advisable—will it save time and labor cost, thus earning the difference in price or will the cost of upkeep be appreciably less? Unless it can be shown to be more economical, its O.K. is doubtful. Favorable reports from other institutional users are valuable.

There are several advantages to a budget. First, the planning involved—the ideas for revising the working schedule (so long postponed) must be carefully worked out to show here; when approved, it makes fewer consultations necessary before buying and the chance to profit by special sales. It establishes aims with both responsibility and authority for carrying them out; and if certain requests are not accepted, it gives opportunity for getting that wider view of planning for the best good of the whole organization, which is needed by every department head.

When buying must be done by the housekeeper, she needs all the help she can get from the various institutional manuals on linens, equipment, the approved list of products used for cleaning, treatment of floors, and all sorts of fiber information, for example. She also must make out definite specifications for some things—all of which is most interesting, but a mistake in choice is her's and sometimes costly. Where there is a purchasing department, this responsibility lies there, though the choice from approved samples should be the housekeeper's, as sanctioned by management, in the case of a large expenditure. Close and agreeable cooperation is necessary for anything less can be most frustrating. Definite specifications and requisitions, with a picture of equipment wanted, and color swatches or samples will be needed in most cases. Any change of product purchased should be approved by the department head.

Forecasts

The use of these is growing steadily for they have proved to be a definite aid to reduced payroll in several departments. If you do not have this system of control, you may probably need to know about it soon, so here is how it works: It is not yet perfect enough to be considered a science but the big accounting firms are hunting for ways to improve it. The appointed Forecast Committee usually consists of an assistant manager, as chairman, the sales manager, maitre d'hotel, housekeeper, engineer, chef, steward and service manager. They meet once a week, usually Friday morning, to discuss the probable house count and functions for the coming week.

The assistant manager has a tentative schedule of occupancy for each day compiled from reservations, guests staying over, records of past years for the same dates, and his information of scheduled local events.

The sales manager adds his estimate of conventions and other business not included in that of the assistant manager. The maitre d'hotel's function list shows reservations in his department, with suggested possibilities of guest rooms required also. The others add any further information they may have of extra events to occur which might increase patronage of dining or bedrooms or both. These are talked over and their estimates combined to forecast the probable number of employees necessary in each department for each day. Perhaps two extra elevator men on Friday and a full staff of bellmen, extra room clerk and waiters, and enough housekeeping help to take care of the week end convention. For example, for the Charity Ball on Wednesday, the engineer will need help to operate the spot light, and a full staff of elevator men and an extra doorman are decided on. Six extra waiters and the public address system are wanted at the Civic Club luncheon on Thursday, etc.

This conference alerts every department head to the week's requirements for each day. The steward knows how much food to buy and when to have it delivered, from the number of reservations and the menus chosen. The chef plans for the help needed each day. The engineer knows the extra work for his staff. The housekeeper must arrange for banquet housemen and the right amount of table linen, as well as for enough workers to take care of the guest rooms. If any changes are made in these arrangements, each department head involved is notified at once. Usually the housekeeper confers with an assistant manager at three o'clock each day to verify the next day's commitments. That gives time to notify employees before they go home if they will not be needed the following morning.

All surplus help must be accounted for and the week's total over or under par shown. Forecasts and actual people on duty are expected

Room Occupancy Forecast
Week of April 21st-27th

Night of Date	Sat 4/21	Sun 4/22	Mon 4/23	Tues 4/24	Wed 4/25	Thurs 4/26	Fri 4/27
Permanents	33	33	33	33	33	33	33
Reservations	154	55	177	209	269	227	150
Anticipated Reservations	203	182	250	238	178	210	217
Total Rooms Forecast	390	270	460	480	480	470	400
Morning Maids Allowed	Sun 24	Mon 18	Tues 28	Wed 32	Thurs 32	Fri 29	Sat 27
Actual House Count	452	223	452	519	522	434	503
Actual Rooms Occupied	325	205	408	479	480	398	411
Over or Under Forecast	-65	-65	-52	-1	O.K.	-72	+11
Maids Allowed	20½	13	25½	30	30	25	26
Maids on Duty	21	20	27	30	28	31	24
TOTAL Over or Under	+½	+7 *	+1½	O.K.	-2	+6 **	-2

WEEK'S TOTAL + 11

* Rooms going in order—216, 404, 1323, 1520. Also getting the State Suite ready for a VIP after a wedding.
** All necessary to clean up the first floor and set it up again after last night's college parties where all the furniture was removed except chairs and tables which were put in.

to balance by the end of the month. No fault is usually found by management if there are fewer people used, but that situation usually is bad from the guests' point of view.

With this strict accounting, it seems that the best way to keep morale high is to have a minimum basic staff, determined by the lowest level of occupancy customary, and hire all others on an hourly basis. An analysis of guest demands for service should govern the hours scheduled for these workers. Instead of extra workers coming in at 8 A.M., it may be better for them and for the housekeeper to plan an earlier or later time. The ones doing the best job will naturally be used to fill vacancies in the regular staff as they come. The number of rooms they can do *satisfactorily* in an hour gives their productivity, on which we base the fitness for advancement.

Today's cost consciousness is responsible for intelligent questioning of every method used in this department so cleaning and sanitation have come in for examination. Sometimes a consultant is called in for recommendations and retraining. Others call on the equipment houses for advice on these things. Both ways can result in appreciable savings making it possible to reduce the maintenance budget.

CHAPTER 16

Cleaning Equipment and Supplies

Heavy duty equipment includes wall washing machines, those for shampooing carpets, vacuum cleaners for wet or dry work, floor polishers, trucks for delivering linen from laundry or linen room to floors and those for carrying mopping utensils; maid's linen carts, and sewing machines.

The kind and amount of cleaning equipment needed will vary with the types of floors and other surfaces to be cleaned and the size of the institution. The small place probably will not need the same size or type of machine and certainly not as many as where large areas must be cleaned or waxed. Comparative tests of efficiency and careful consideration of the merits of each should determine the type best suited to the particular house.

Most institutions have a variety of floors; marble, terrazzo, hard or soft wood; and coverings—carpet, linoleum, rubber, vinyl or asphalt tile. Any or all may be used and each presents its own problem of maintenance and the equipment needed to care for it. For information as to the right one for each, ask the manufacturer or Trade Association of the floor or covering to be cleaned what they recommend and the best method for its use. The various Institutional Associations also have valuable manuals on these subjects.

Since daily vacuuming is advised by carpet manufacturers, it is wise to look over the various types before buying—even better to have them demonstrated in your own establishment. There are new types being shown and each has certain improvements. The various types include the upright with motor driven brush, the tank, the cylinder type which lies on the floor, the drum tank, the one to sling over the shoulder, the small hand one, and the light weight electric broom. Before buying one, it is wise to decide:

1. For what purpose it will be used—carpets only or for high dusting, draperies, venetian blinds, mattresses, springs, or bare floors?
2. If it is to be used daily, what is the probable length of time you can expect for efficient service?
3. Is it heavy and difficult to handle or so light weight that it will break easily?
4. How many of its attachments will be used often? Are they included in the price quoted or must you buy them separately?
5. Is it made by a reputable firm? For how long guaranteed? Where can you get repairs made or replacements when needed?
6. Is it easily cleaned?
7. How noisy is it?
8. Is it approved by your chief engineer whose men will take care of it?

The prevalent opinion is that a carpet washing machine, used by a properly trained houseman, is less expensive than having it done by an outsider. In some places where this work is seasonal, it has been paid for by renting to smaller places near by during the off season, along with the regular houseman who operates it.

There are also various kinds of mops, brooms, brushes, squeegees, chamois (or a substitute), sponges and pails, to name only a few things needed to keep a clean house. Cleaning supplies will include the polishes for floors, furniture, and metals. All should be tested and when a satisfactory one is found which is approved by others in the same work, is reasonable in price and easy to get in the quantities needed, it is a good idea to keep using it until convinced that a new product is *really* more effective, costs no more and for which quick delivery is assured. This does not mean one must "be the last by whom the new is tried" but only careful about a change to a new product until convinced it is better in every way. One very good reason for not rushing into the use of new things is the resistance of employees to new products They must be sold on its advantage to *them*. Is it easier on their hands? Does it get quicker results or make the work easier for them in some way? One way used for selling them is to ask one of the most popular maids to try it out, as you are not quite sure if it is as good as that which is being used. Explain what the salesman claims and ask if she will see if it is true. If she likes it, it is much easier to sell the others. With metal cleaners and polishes, be very careful to read the label and do not buy one containing poison, for employees are very apt to be careless in its use. Anything having a low combustion point is dangerous—a real fire hazard and anything so highly volatile that evaporation increases the amount to be bought annually is, of course, too expensive.

Disinfectants, Soaps, and Detergents

All cleaners should be as mild as possible, for the good of hands and the surface cleaned. The finish on many new porcelain fixtures is needlesly worn off by the use of a cleaner that is too abrasive. Where the fixture is already old and worn, it may need the harsher treatment to get it clean, but the new one usually responds to gentler handling. Use the multi-purpose cleaner as a time-saver whenever possible. It also prevents confusion about which one to use and is less expensive because it can be purchased in larger quantities. Today there is no need for a cleaner with a strong or unpleasant odor, as indicated by the absence of that former "hospital smell."

Storage and Distribution

This is a very important part of any control system, but when one person, carefully chosen and trained, is definitely in charge of and responsible for the receipt, storage, and distribution of equipment and supplies, there is little chance for things to go astray. The storage place may be only large enough for a week's supply of the department's needs. The person in charge gets the first assistant's signature on the order for that amount from General Stores and leaves with her the records of things issued for the preceding week. He takes inventory once a month and this shows what was on hand at the beginning of the month, what was received, and what issued during this time and the balance on hand. The first assistant checks this before okaying the next month's order. Records of receipts and issues are kept in books of different colored paper.

There should be marked shelves or sections on which the designated items are always kept, thus saving time in looking for them, and it is easier to keep track of them. A daily record of the employees using equipment is needed, so that anyone having repairs too often can be retrained in the use of it. There will also be certain specified amounts of each cleaning material given out daily to the floor sections and attention called to requests for either too much or too little. If a full time attendant is not needed, the man can be assigned other duties or a part time worker employed for certain hours. In one place, a young man studying Hotel Management was used for certain hours before his college classes began and on Saturdays, when he took stock and cleaned the storeroom.

Safety precautions are important here also. All stock must be kept at least 18 inches below the ceiling and sprinkler system; no smoking allowed; a fire extinguisher in good order kept here and a built in metal box used for storing matches Adequate aisle spaces are needed for trucking things in; shelves should not be wider than necessary for each product and drawers not longer than 15 inches, deeper than 12 inches or more than 20 inches from front to back. Some storerooms have narrow shelving on the walls, with a double stack in the center. Drums of liquid should be kept on raised platforms with detachable ramp for putting them in place.

Part IV

FURNISHINGS, THEIR PURCHASES AND CARE

CHAPTER 17

Hotel Table Linen

Before the World Wars, all good hotels used only linen napery and many of the higher priced ones had only linen face towels, but the government's demand for a fiber with high tensile strength to use in parachute harness, fire hose and many other things, made it necessary for manufacturers to find substitutes. This resulted in a durable cotton damask of excellent design, so finished that linting was greatly reduced. Their continued experiments have produced an even finer quality and a minimum of linting, in colors as well as white. Another Jacquard loom product is woven from a mixture of long stapled Egyptian cotton and rayon or other man-made fibers, having a high luster. "Mummy cloth" and other lint free special weaves, which can be dyed in beautiful colors, printed with attractive designs or a crest are still popular—especially for informal rooms, and wherever the budget will not permit a good quality of linen. The decoration of many very attractive dining rooms is enhanced by the use of colorful table cloths and napkins.

Printed designs may be applied by means of etched copper rollers hand blocked or hand screened. The machine process is the fastest and cheapest as it can be used on large quantities of material before blurring. It is necessary for the color to be fast, as cloths must be washed with the regular stock, to avoid extra laundry expense. Also, when stained it must be bleached. When a hand-cut wooden block is used by applying one color at a time by band, it is much more expensive, but the most costly process is that of screen printing by hand because only a limited number can be done before the silk screen wears out. These are truly luxury items for they cannot stand bleaching, and therefore are not practical.

Where the budget will permit its use, most of the better hotels have pure linen in their formal dining rooms. Many of them have found that a different kind and color for each type of room where food is sold, is not only less expensive, but increases the control of this costly article by fixing the responsibility for its loss on the managers of the rooms.

Most of the napery bought by institutions is *single damask* weave cotton. This term means that the filling threads are woven alternately over one warp thread and under five, with from 140 to 175 threads per inch, giving good wearing qualities for institutional use. Designs are likely to be small and because of the close weave, even the satin band in a pattern is not apt to get fuzzy. A permanent finish is usual to retain sheen and prevent shedding but this should not be one which holds chlorine because napkins often, and clothes sometimes, need to be bleached to remove stains.

Double damask is not necessarily thicker or stronger than the single. The term means only a difference in weave, and often a finer thread. In this damask the weft thread alternately overlaps seven warp threads and binds in the eighth. This makes a firm cloth, gives the pattern a solid effect and adds to the luster. It is always more expensive than the single and to be worth the higher price must be closely woven of fine threads. From 200 to 300 threads to the square inch is a popular quality for hotels, clubs, and motels. Few other institutions use double damask, except for special occasions. This kind of table linen can also be had in colors, and a plain weave is obtainable with stripes, plaids, or borders. Be sure it is labelled "Guaranteed Fast Color." For specifications of suitable quality in this fabric, it is advisable to consult *Performance Requirements for Table Linen* in "The Hotel Textile Purchasing Guide," available from the American Hotel Association. Be sure to consult label for fiber content—"Linen 60%, cotton 40%" or the opposite, indicating whether you are getting what was ordered.

Sizes

The table set ups in the different dining rooms will determine the sizes necessary. The usual ones are:

Tops, and for deuces—45" x 45".

Cloths—54" x 54", 63" x 63", and 72" x 72".

Banquet cloths for long tables—72" x 90" and 90" x 108".

Banquet cloths for round tables—81" x 81", 90" x 90", and
   108" x 108".
Napkins are usually 22" x 22" or 20" x 20" in formal rooms for
   dinner.
For breakfast, lunch or banquets—18" x 18" or the 12" x 20" half
   napkin, which is less bulky and also costs less. This change depends on patron acceptance.
For tea—12" x 12" are usual, often in plain linen.

Amount

A "three par" in circulation is customary with one-half par in the
linen room for use as needed, when the laundry works a five-day week.
This means three times the average of each item used in a busy week.
The three and one-half times the par stock carefully used on alternate
days lengthens the life of linens by allowing for rest between washings. After receiving the proper amount of desired quality, intelligent
care must be used to get the best returns from investment in this
expensive material. In Chapter 14, on Controls we spoke of the
proper storage or reserve stock. It is equally important to take the
right kind of care of that in circulation. Some suggestions were made
in Chapter 3, where the combined responsibilities of housekeeper
and managers of all rooms serving food were discussed. Here are a
few more ways of prolonging the life of linen: (1) Dropping large
bundles of it down the linen chute, not only wastes time in sorting
but rubbing against the sides of the chute causes unnecessary wear.
(2) Diners can be prevented from using the tablecloth for drawing
(with knife, fork or pencil) an illustration of a project under dis-
cussion by a wide-awake waiter or bus boy's offer of the previous
day's menu (if the back is unprinted) or a large pad may be kept in
the room for that use. (3) Everyone who handles table linen must
be impresed with its cost and the necessity for its care. Unceasing
and strict vigilance is the only way to prevent abuses.

Laundering

Laundry methods affect the life of linen greatly. Removing stains
before washing and separating the badly soiled for special treatment
prevents the use of bleaches where they are not needed. A mild soap

with no free alkali and as little bleach as possible is recommended. Table linens must be thoroughly rinsed in soft water. Some manufacturers recommend a bit of powdered borax in the bluing water. Very little starch should be used and damask should be ironed while moist and allowed to dry well before using. Continuous ironing on the some fold will wear that line out too soon.

Shortages

Napkins are lost more often than any other pieces of table linen because men often thoughtlessly put them in their pockets and women take home the table decorations in them. Many hotels are following the example of clubs and removing napkins with the last course. This custom shows a definite decrease in loss. We have mentioned the use of different colors in each room as a way of detecting where loss occurs. Wherever possible the even exchange system should be used as it is at present the best control method. If an outside laundry is used, crest woven pieces reduce loss.

Rental Linen Service

This type of linen service is becoming increasingly popular, especially with motels and smaller hotels. The reasons given are: There is no worry over laundry operations; no investment in reserve stock of linens or laundry equipment; and, where costs are reasonable and service good, it is an advantage. The pros and cons of this system are capably treated in L. A. Bradley's book mentioned before. One of the universities has operated a rental service for four years and found it satisfactory, so larger hotels, already having laundries large enough, are considering this possible way to add to income.

CHAPTER 18

Bed and Bath Linen

Thorough and accurate information on room linens is necessary for the executive housekeeper, as at least one and a half cents of every dollar of room revenue is spent on this one item. Both quality and quantity need careful consideration. The former should be the best the budget will allow which is suitable for the type of operation. Quantity depends on the size of the house, number, kind, and size of beds, and the standard setup—whether two, three, or four sheets are used on a bed (one extra to cover the blanket, the other to cover the spring) ; if two, four or six face or bath towels and how many face cloths are the rule. The knowledge of what amount of new linen of each kind used is in the reserve stock room and the amount and condition of that in circulation, also governs the annual expenditure.

It used to be considered that a three par stock was sufficient for circulation—one in the room, another in the laundry being washed, and a third in linen closets—but today this is not true *if* the laundry (in or out of the place) works only a five-day week and the week-ends are apt to be busy. At least one-half par is needed for the week-end and many institutions find a full four par is best. It is a fact that constant use and laundering wear linens out more quickly than when it has a "rest period." Shortage of linen makes a poor impression on patrons, adds to the work of maids in going back to the room with supplies they should have had when making it up and as stated, makes for unnecessary purchase.

Room Set-Ups

To determine the number of pieces of each kind needed, multiply the standard set-up for each room by the number of rooms and that amount by three and one-half or four, whichever "par" has been approved. To illustrate, let us take a four par. The hotel has 100 twin beds with two sheets to a bed, that make 800—one set on the beds, one in laundry, one in closets ready to go on beds and the fourth in the linen room ready to use on call. There are 50 large beds, each with two sheets—a total of one hundred to make them up. Four times that is 400. For pillow cases one on each twin or single bed is 100, plus two on each large bed—200 cases for one setup and 800 in circulation. Use the same system for each kind of towel and for face cloths. The standard for bedpads, blankets, spreads, tub mats, bath rugs, and shower sheets need not be so large. A two and a half to three par is usually enough, as they are not all changed daily. When reckoning the number of these needed for four par, you may think it a large amount, but replacement cost is appreciably lower than if too short a supply is used. Naturally size, kind, and amount needed for the low price commercial house will differ from that in the luxury city or resort Hotel where guest appeal is the criterion.

Room Linen

Sheet Sizes and Quality

Size is as important as quality in choosing sheets, for too small a size will annoy the client if he has to keep pulling the top one over his shoulders. It also wears out faster and cannot be tucked in properly at sides or foot of bed. They should be large enough to tuck the bottom sheet in securely all the way around and for the top one to be held securely at the bottom, with a top 8″ turnover for blanket protection. The best sizes: 72″ x 108″ for twin beds— 90″ x 108″ for double bed, 63″ x 99″ for cots, and 108″ x 108″ for the large bed which is becoming increasingly popular. The 108″ is cut length before the three inch top and two inch lower hems are made. Six per cent is usually allowed for shrinkage, so the 108″ makes a sheet actually 98″ when finished.

Cut length	108″
Hems	5″
	103″
Shrinkage	5″
Length after Laundering	98″

The 98" finished length is needed for bottom sheets because:

The standard mattress length is		76" to 80"
The standard mattress thickness for turnover	6" to 8" top	
The standard mattress thickness for turnover	6" to 8" bottom	12" to 16"
	12" for both	
Tucked under at top and bottom	10" to 14"	10" to 14"
Top sheet the same for turning over		98" to 110"

So, for the "giant size"—increasingly necessary for the tall people—the manufacturers are making the big sheets to fit, even up to 108 x 120, if mattress is still thicker. These largest ones are usually made in percale only. Many buyers consider it more economical to have hems made the same at top and bottom—two and one-half inches—so as to avoid the constant shoulder wear at one end.

Fitted lower sheets for hotels, clubs, and motels are increasing in popularity as manufacturers are strengthening the mitered corners, which are the first place to tear. They are lighter in weight, an advantage when laundry cost is governed by that factor; beds are made more quickly, look neater, when not changed daily and the first cost is less than flat ones. The fitted nylon tricot ones can be tumble dried, saving cost of ironing and all nylon fitted sheets except those of nylon-acetate are stronger than cotton. The disadvantages to fitted sheets are: (1) they pose a problem for laundries when ironing the mitered corners; (2) maids must be trained to be careful in putting them on and pulling them off to avoid tearing; (3) they take up almost twice as much shelf space as flat ones; and (4) it is more difficult to fold them. Since nylon fitted sheets dry so quickly and last longer, it can mean less capital tied up in bedding. It is not advisable to use both top and bottom nylon sheets because the top one tends to slide off the body, when a person turns. Some people do not care for nylon cases because of the slippery feeling. Again the reaction of guests is a deciding factor in the choice. One manufacturer now advertises "elastic corners" and another has elastic across top and bottom as well as at corners for greater ease in putting them on.

These are characteristics of good sheets:

1. *Count*—which is a customary specification. This may vary from 128, the minimum number of threads per square inch, through 140 to 180 for carded cotton sheeting, and 180 to 200 for combed percale. Few institutions, buy the 128 today because it wears out more quickly. Cotton and percale sheets wear almost equally well for hotels, clubs, and motels but schools, colleges, and especially hospitals (where bleaches are constantly used for all sorts of stains) find the one which costs less to buy and wears at least equally well is best for their purpose. Percale appeals to guests because of its smoothness, and costs less for laundry if the charge is by weight. When it is laundered in the house, its lighter weight also allows more sheets in a load, so decreases the number of loads and thus the cost, still further.

2. *Weave*—A durable sheet is closely woven and well balanced—not much difference in warp and woof threads. Hold the fabric to the light to see this and also any imperfections—possibly knots or thin places, which makes the cloth a "second."

3. *Sizing*—Best grades need little sizing. Test for it by rubbing between the thumbs over a dark material. If much starch falls, hold it to the light again and you will probably find it is loosely woven, hence, not durable.

4. *Selvage*—A "cape" selvage is best. That means it has extra threads woven in along the edge for strength.

5. *Workmanship*—Hems should have small, even stitches, 10 to 12 to the inch and hem ends also stitched to prevent raveling.

6. *Tensile Strength*—The amount of strain it takes to break the fabric. This must be stated on the label. The 24 standards before mentioned will give the minimum for all counts, as well as all other information needed for buying guidance. It is wise to buy well known brands from reputable concerns to be sure of getting what you want. Remember that most manufacturers make several grades so be sure to specify the brand name which meets your specifications. Decide these points and your ordering is much easier.

Kinds of Sheets

We have mentioned cotton (sometimes called muslin) and percale sheets, but have not indicated the chief difference—the percales have gone through an extra process, combing, after carding, and this removes the short fibers to make the fabric smoother. Naturally this extra labor increases the cost but we have seen how it pays for this by its additional qualities of being lighter than cotton, yet wearing as well. It also irons easily, stays white and get silkier every time it is washed—up to 400 or 450 times. If the initial cost of percale is beyond the budget or not required by the type of institution, a good quality of muslin is satisfactory. The 140 count sheet, for instance, will stand 360 to 400 washings *if* it has a chance to rest between times. Apartment hotels, especially, like the fitted or contour sheets, as daily change of bed linen is not customary except in the luxury type of operation. We have considered their benefits and disadvantages except for mentioning that a top fitted sheet, having only one end fitted does not look well when only tumble dried.

Colored Sheets

These became so very popular that the American Hotel Association had a series of tests made in different parts of the country by its Housekeeping Committee as to color fastness, durability, and guest reactions. All met requirements and many hotels and motels are using them with satisfaction.

Pillow Cases

These are made of sheeting, so the same considerations govern their choice. Many establishments which cannot afford percale sheets do buy this quality of cases because of the extra softness and smoothness which guests appreciate so much. Size is important, as too tight a case, not allowing for the amount of shrinkage, will be strained every time it is put on a pillow. On the other hand one too large, costs more than necessary and does not look well. The accepted allowance is from 6" to 8" longer than the pillow the latter for percale cases with 4" hems, and 2" to 4" more than its circumference. Feather pillows range from 19″ x 25″ to 22″ x 28″. Down often are 17″ x 27″, while foam rubber ones vary from 15″ x 26″ to 20″ x 27″. Here smaller size cases are better. The prevalent use of night creams and hair óil require bleach for cases, so this may be the deciding factor in choosing the less costly muslin rather than percale cases.

Bed Pads

These are used to protect the mattress, save wear on sheets (especially where mattresses are tufted or tied or have buttons) and to add to guest comfort. They may be flat or fitted with elastic corner bands; of foam latex, plastic foam, covered with sheeting or not; quilted sanforized muslin filled with cotton, nylon or a combination of the two; or of a felt like material guaranteed washable without shrinking if directions are followed. The quilted ones are nearly all sanforized, so larger than mattress sizes are not necessary.

Blankets

Only the finest wool can be used for white blankets, so they are expensive but many luxury hotels feel they are worth the price for the guest satisfaction they give. Many places use colored ones that carry out the color scheme and have found that light ones clean well. Their popularity over dark ones seems to stem from an idea that dark ones hide soil, so may not be completely clean. Silk, rayon, or sateen bindings have replaced stitched edges almost entirely. Crested blankets are believed to prevent loss. All wool blankets are still popular, as they are warm, durable, and come in truly beautiful colors, but the advantage of some man-made fiber ones lies in their moth proof quality and very light weight which makes them useable in warm weather. Hence the need for less storage space. For twin beds the common sizes are 60″ x 84″ or 72″ x 90″ with 72″ x 84″ or 80″ x 90″ for large beds.

Cotton blankets are used in many parts of the country practically the year round and increasingly as night spreads. They are necessarily color fast and machine printed in interesting designs and beautiful colors.

Bed Spreads

As a part of room decor, these are now varied in color and fabric. In expensive establishments, they may be made of satin, nylon, other synthetic fiber materials or blends with silk. Medium and low priced institutions find cotton, chenille or corduroy—plain, striped or figured less costly and just as satisfactory. Sizes vary from the old standard of 72" x 108" for twin beds and 90" x 108" for double beds to much longer and wider ones as chosen by the decorator.

BATH LINEN

Face and Hand Towels

Quality, sizes and fiber are governed by the budget and type of operation. The face towel may be anywhere from 17" x 32" to 26" x 40"—a popular size, or even larger. It may be all linen, damask or huck weave, linen and cotton huck, or all cotton huck. The label must tell the fiber content and the first named is the largest proportion used. Some of the better hotels continue the use of sizeable pure linen damask face towels, as they are not only the most beautiful but are highly absorbent, do not lint, are very durable because the flax fibers are long and strong. They launder well and get softer and smoother with age, as do the all linen huck face towels. This type is stronger because of its firmer weave and it is often name woven either in border or center. Sometimes a combination of these are placed in the same bath, with the hand towels of huck and face of damask. The majority of hotels, clubs and motels use a firmly woven huck face towel made of tightly twisted linen and cotton yarns for it keeps its color and wears well. These are often name woven through the center or in the border, sometimes in color. The all cotton huck towel, though strong and much less expensive, is not as satisfactory for it stains more easily, is not quite as absorbent and is apt to lint. It also is likely to look grey with use unless bleached often. Sizes vary from 17" x 32" to 20" x 40", with 18" x 36" the most popular. Where hand towels are used, they are usually of huck, or in some places match bath towels, to save laundry costs. Sizes run from 15" x 25" to 18" x 28".

Bath Towels

These are ordinarily made of all cotton in a terry or ribbed weave. The latter is popular in athletic clubs, turkish baths and in college and school athletic field houses because it gives more friction and outwears the other kind, of equal price. These facts are increasing its demand in other places. All-white bath towels are considered more absorbent than colored because the latter have already assimilated dye. The difference is not great and many establishments use colored towels as a decorative feature in baths.

The best bath towels are made of a high grade cotton, evenly spun with many loops held in a closely woven background fabric, in which warp and woof threads are of almost equal strength. If too loosely woven, the loops pull out too easily. If there is any difference in strength of threads, the warp should be stronger as most of the pulling strain is on them. Whether long or short loops are used (largely dictated by fashion) they must be close for greatest absorption. The loop made of two threads is a bit stronger, of course. Holding the towel to the light will show if weave is tight or loose.

Selvage should be at least one-fourth inches wide and firmly woven for double strength but if it shrinks more than the rest of the towel it does not look well. This problem is being worked on now by the big manufacturers because at present the selvage is where the towel often gives out first. Hems should have small stitches and be back stitched at the ends to prevent raveling. Sizes range from 20" x 40" to 25" x 50", with 22" x 44" and 24" x 46" the most popular. Where hand towels and face cloths are standard, the former may be terry cloth in sizes 11" x 18" to 16" x 28". Face cloths range from 11" x 11" to 13" x 13". Any or all of these may be name woven where and as desired.

Shower Curtains

These come in several different materials—all with plus and minus traits.

1. White or colored duck is sturdy, launders well and any mildew can be bleached out with care. It is not commonly used in the

better places unless in shower stalls because of its weight and the trend for bathroom decoration.

2. Plastic sheeting offers the chance for color and design but needs reinforced grommets, weighted hem, and tends to stick together if not dried well.

3. For luxury operations mildew resistant nylon curtains are popular as they come in beautiful colors and designs. They last better when a clear plastic one is used with them as a lining.

CHAPTER 19

Springs, Mattresses and Pillows

Springs

There are still three kinds of bed springs in use though the box spring is the most popular. It is also the easiest to keep clean because it is fully covered and takes less time for vacuuming. The felt-upholstered top adds to its comfort and durability.

Many small institutions and camps still use the coil spring with a hair or cotton felt mattress. Flat springs are of three types, the cable wire spring, the metal band, and the open coils. Their initial cost is lower and they are used largely for roll-away cots and dormitory beds.

Mattresses

The rubber foam mattress is increasingly popular for institutional use because of its comfort for those who do not want a hard mattress. It does not have to be turned and its ticking can be zipped on and taken off easily for washing. There is a wide difference of opinion as to the comparative coolness of this kind and the innerspring. It is only about half as thick as the innerspring mattress, and if a fitted sheet is to be used, the size of the sheet must be specified.

The innerspring mattress is still the best seller. The kind with the coils fastened together with metal ties and those in which the coils are put in cloth pockets which are sewed together, are both popular, but the latter are more durable. The top and bottom padding is what largely determines the comfort and, to some extent, the durability of the mattress. This is usually curled hair or felted cotton, or a mixture of the two. To deal with a reputable concern is vitally important when buying both mattress and springs for cheap materials and poor workmanship can all too easily be hidden by a smart looking covering.

All extra mattresses should be stored on slatted shelves for ventilation. These shelves should be of the same width as the mattress. No more than ten inches between shelves is necessary. This system adds to their length of service. If they are piled one on top of the other, the weight on the lower ones is too great.

Pillows

As with mattresses, pillows of rubber foam suit many people. They have the same merits and faults as do mattresses. Dacron pillows are comparatively new and evidently increasing in popularity, especially with those who suffer from an allergy to feathers. Their washability is a practical factor in their general acceptance by the public. Plenty of people still like feather pillows best. Except for the down "baby pillows" liked by those who want very little under their heads, a mixture of down and either goose or duck or a high grade all-goose feather pillow is considered durable and holds its resiliency well.

It is well to have on hand a few of each kind of mattresses and pillows for the guests who request them and also to be prepared to answer calls for plastic pillow covers and bed boards.

CHAPTER 20

Selection and Repair of Furniture and Floor Coverings

Today the labor cost of maintaining the large number of pieces of very ornate furniture once used in hotel rooms would be terrific. Hence, the work has been simplified by the use of fewer pieces of simpler design, often of light wood that does not show every fingerprint. The demand is also made on the manufacturers for stain and burn proof finishes as well. Experience has shown the expense of frequent recovering of chairs with upholstered arm and backs high enough to absorb the hair dye or oil. Hence the modified Morris chair type is now being used. The lower back and wooden arms decrease definitely the necessity for recovering the chair so often and it costs less to reupholster cushions than the entire chair. The best models are very comfortable as well.

Some of the new plastic materials are beautiful and a great help in keeping upholstered pieces clean and fresh looking at little labor cost. Other materials woven from fibers protectively finished are easily kept clean also.

Where slipcovers are used, the material should, of course, be both tub and sun fast and preshrunk. They should never be made skin tight, however. Replacing them on the furniture when only the pleats are bone dry stretches them into shape.

There are still people who want the high back and upholstered arm pieces so there should be some of those available on request. A piece of thin, colorless plastic, like that used for keeping vegetables fresh, should be placed by the upholsterer between the muslin cover and the covering material on the back and arms. This will prevent stains from soaking into the muslin cover and will make cleaning much easier and more effective. Matching arm and head slipcover pieces can be removed for cleaning as desired.

We find that chairs with slanted back legs which prevent contact with the wall, reduce wall washing to such an extent that we are hoping all other pieces of furniture may soon be designed and made in the same way, especially trunk racks. Unfortunately not all of the new designs are work savers. One piece to be avoided because of the time needed for proper dusting is the slat-top coffee table. Today's light wood furniture with labor-saving finishes is so much more attractive and easy to care for than the old kind, that renovating the old is advisable only when it is of excellent quality, structurally suitable, and in such good condition that only styling is needed to make it up-to-date. When stain and burn resistant tops are used this is an added labor saver.

It is wise to replace dresser mirrors with one the full width of the dresser hung on the wall. Where there is room for two dressers to be placed side by side for a "Mr. and Mrs." effect, the mirror should be the full width of both dressers. Some furniture renovation companies are joining desk, dresser, TV and baggage rack very effectively. Be sure to have enough with the desk at the right of the dresser and others at the left to fit the demands of the wall spaces.

The studio bed or day-bed type is being widely used in hotels but they are finding that some guests do not like them. In addition, pulling them out for making up wears out the carpet and maids complain of backaches if there are too many in a section, so most places have beds of each type available—double, twin, and couch beds.

Where hotels have their own repair shops, they can conserve time and labor by saving all good parts of broken tables and chairs and storing them in open wall bins. When an arm or leg is broken, it can be replaced quickly by one of the same type. This system is used at the Hotel Statler in Boston. If mattress tufts are replaced by the upholsterer, there is a tuft available for speedy and satisfactory use.

It is standard practice in most places to tag all furniture sent from rooms for repair or refinishing with the date and room number. If the room is out of order, the tag also bears the date on which the article will be needed for putting the room back in order.

Floor Coverings

How to care for, clean and repair carpets is important because of their expense. Fortunately, there is a wealth of informative material available, starting with the U. S. Department of Agriculture Farmers' Bulletin #1960, "Carpet and Rug Repair." The American Hotel Association has an excellent bulletin. Every large carpet concern offers valuable advice and the carpet cleaning equipment firms also give information on methods of cleaning them according to the fiber content.

Wool carpets were formerly the only ones used, but now we have wool mixed with man-made fibers or made from them alone, as in nylon carpets. We also use cotton, linen, and a mixture of the two. Hence, it is necessary to understand the care of all the different kinds we have in use. For this, our safest method is to depend on what the manufacturers tell us to do.

Carpet Cleaning

All nylon, made especially for planes, is definitely easy to spot-clean from coffee stains with plain soap and water. Protein stains made by air sick passengers are removed as easily and in addition, the nylon being smooth instead of notched like wool, is very soil resistant. Soap and water, carbon tetrachloride, or benzene, remove dirt or grease stains easily. Since nylon absorbs only one-third as much water as wool, it dries much faster after shampooing.

Those annoying spots that new carpets acquire from misuse by regular guests, conventions, and meetings, can't wait for a scheduled monthly or quarterly cleaning time, and a spot removal kit is a worthwhile investment. In it should be the various things needed for different sorts of stains.

The container can be an aluminum basket and the worker should always be furnished with white blotting paper and discarded tub mats or bath towels for absorbing extra moisture. If the house is large enough so that a man is used daily for carpet washing, he should be the one to do this work, or else the person in charge of upholstery cleaning.

The National Institute of Rug Cleaners urges promptness of treatment. The results of accidents by babies or puppies should be sponged at once with lukewarm water. Then mix a teaspoonful of white vinegar with three teaspoonsful of water and sponge this on. Rinse and blot up the excess moisture with clean, unstarched rags. When this is dry, wash the area with a teaspoonful of soapless detergent dissolved in a half-pint of warm water. Rinse and blot excess water.

A spilled beverage or fruit juice (especially if it contains sugar), is another signal for clean-up action. Again, the warm-water sponging is the quickest, most effective treatment. Wise precaution is to follow up with a detergent solution, rinse, and blot up excess moisture.

For greasy stains, the National Institute of Rug Cleaners recommend squirting the carpet with a nonflammable household cleaning fluid or using an eyedropper and sponging up the stain with a dry, white cloth.

Keep on hand a can of a rug-cleaning compound, which is essentially sawdust impregnated with a special cleaning fluid, for grease spots, ink blots, or puzzling stains. A small handful of this cleaner brushed on the stain, allowed to dry thoroughly, then vacuumed usually banishes the offender.

When there is a large stain or one that doesn't respond to mild treatment, the spot should not be rubbed or scrubbed but a professional cleaner called immediately.

For other floor coverings, such as rubber tile, cork, asphalt tile, linoleum or vinyl tile, use only the cleaners and methods advised by the manufacturers. Each group has its own Association or Institute from whom full information as to approved products and techniques can be learned.

Part V

PRINCIPLES OF DECORATION

CHAPTER 21

Scale and Balance

There are a few principles of decoration that every executive housekeeper ought to know as she is accountable for day to day upkeep. By using her wits she can acquire knowledge of decorating fundamentals which will keep the rooms fairly presentable until money is available for a complete renovation job.

By scale we mean the relative proportion of furniture to the size and height of the room and its architectural features. The use of the room is also a factor. A ballroom, lobby, or main dining room would probably take furniture on a larger scale than the informal lounge, parlor, or bedroom.

Balance is the visual effect of furniture arrangement. We have all seen rooms that made us feel they were tilting to one side or one end because all the heavy furniture was concentrated there. We have also seen rooms where the tall pieces were all on one side. Both of these out-of-balance effects are distressing to a guest even though he may not realize why.

Color balance is also important. In nature, the earth is darker than trees or shrubs, while the sky is still lighter. It is a good idea for the novice to plan the darkest color for the floor, lighter walls, and a pale tint or white for the ceiling. Many professional decorators can upset all the rules and get a satisfactory effect, but it takes a real artist to do this.

Choice of Furniture Styles

Good taste and common sense are needed when choosing furniture for institutional use. What would be suitable for the luxury resort or for the country inn would be far from right for the busy commercial hotel. "Functionalism" is an overworked word today, but it does describe what must be the criterion for selecting the furniture for hotels, clubs, and hospitals.

Comfort is one of the things that every hotel guest demands and its meaning differs with the individual, so there must be variety in the setup—rooms with each kind of bed, hard, soft and medium mattresses, rubber and feather pillows.

All guests agree, however, on certain fundamentals: (1) comfortable easy chairs, one for each guest. If space does not permit a second easy chair, be sure that the occasional chair is very comfortable. (2) They want the chairs needed for room service meals unless the dressing table or trunk bench is "sittable"; (3) They expect good lighting for all purposes; (4) draperies and shades easy to arrange for darkening the room when they want to sleep late; (5) adequate work space on the desk. If the length of the desk is 30 inches or less, there should be a drop-leaf to put up when needed. (6) Sizeable mirrors are expected, low enough to see the bottom of a lady's dress and high enough for the tallest man. (7) The bedside table should be large enough to hold the things the *guest* wants to put there as well as the lamp, phone, telephone books, ash tray, and advertising matter. Many have found the step table satisfactory, especially where floor space is limited. (8) Plenty of good-sized ash trays help greatly in avoiding burns on furniture and rugs. (9) Metal wastebaskets are practical fire preventives and can be highly decorative or pleasantly inconspicuous as preferred.

Rooms should give the effect of beauty, comfort, and new style trends. Fortunately, the new furniture is definitely suited for the strenuous treatment it gets from the general public—the large, strong coffee table with stain-proof top; the sizeable couch and chair upholstered in soil-proof or easily cleaned materials and large lamps and pictures, all for use in large rooms. Furniture of light woods makes a small room look larger, and when lightweight, it is easier to move but it must be strongly made to withstand hard wear.

The new finishes are all easily cleaned with a damp cloth instead of needing a polisher's treatment and are also liquor and perfume proof. These qualities, with the additional multi-purpose pieces to reduce dusting time and moving of furniture are all work simplifiers and therefore, lessen labor cost.

The best designs of all styles combine well if the scale is similar and any kinds of wood may be used together if of similar basic design.

CHAPTER **22**

Color and Design

The ABC of hotel decoration, is suitability—fitting the decor to place, use, and budget. There must be beauty of line, materials, and color. Without this a room is dead, but with it there can be created an atmosphere of warm welcome that attracts and holds the guest. This impression of "Make yourself at home, we're glad you're here," should start at first sight of the outside of the building.

A modernized entrance must be set off by a clean sidewalk, sparkling glass and metal, smart uniforms on doorman and bellboy. The lobby must add to that first impression with its clean, cheerful, comfortable, up-to-date appearance. In these days there are durable, easy-to-clean materials in bright colors for use here. Is the elevator up to the mark or is it a dismal spot? Are the corridor carpets worn? The walls dingy or soiled? Everybody going into a room sees this. Even without windows, color and lighting can make it bright and gay.

Then comes the bedroom or suite—a grand finale or a great disappointment? "Guest appeal" is an overworked term but how else can you express the result for which the hotel aims?

Color and Fabrics

In the bedrooms a relaxing, soothing effect is desired, conducive to rest and sleep. So we pass over the extremes of color, the attention-demanding, "geometric" design and choose instead softer tones for the walls, the harmonizing floor covering, upholstery and draperies so that we get a modern effect without that strident demand for attention. The most satisfactory bedrooms are calm and serene, yet each should have a brilliant color note.

Though there are delightful monotone bedrooms most people prefer a bit of color for cheer. This can be added in lampshades, pictures, covered headboards, pillows, the material on a desk chair or by gay upholstery on a small occasional chair. Since beds occupy a large proportion of the floor space, certain decorators keep spreads closely allied to carpet or wall color. Others think the spread the logical place for the splash of brilliant hue, since it is removed at night.

Color can do so many things. It can improve the proportions of a room by making it appear larger or smaller; it can raise or lower the ceiling, or by using the same paint on everything, it can minimize bad structural defects. Make use of these ideas when needed.

The newest fabrics have all kinds of wonderful qualities. They are sun- and tub-fast, fire-resistant, moth- and mildew-proof, dirt resistant, etc. The new designs and colors are beautiful also. We've "never had it so good' if we use care in choosing and test the fabrics before buying.

Manufacturers of all fabrics, including carpets, are working unceasingly to overcome defects in them, so watch advertising for results. For instance, when they first came out, fiberglass fabrics were not very easy to drape but hung straight and stiff from the top pleats. Today there are the softest, easiest-to-drape fabrics of this material, obtainable in sheer, medium, or heavy textures. Glass curtains made of it were easily washable and smart looking, but they were brittle to a certain extent, so that friction of any kind, if continued, caused broken threads and the fabric did not look well mended. These drawbacks of the use of glass fabrics have been largely rectified and they are becoming increasingly popular.

We might go through a list of materials to show how they have improved but it is not necessary to emphasize the changes still to come. This example alone shows how foolish it is to think *any* disadvantage will be permanent. All manufacturers will welcome questions as to qualities you find unsatisfactory. Do not hesitate to ask your salesman also. He may be able to tell you when to expect a new fiber or finishing treatment which removes the fault.

The designs get more beautiful all the time and the new weaves and finishes are appearing so fast that we have only to get an idea of something we think would be better than what we have and lo! it is available. "We have never had it so good," if we choose and test carefully.

Furniture Arrangement

Arrangement of furniture is important. It should be placed for comfort. If you find chairs and tables rearranged every time a suite is occupied, it's a sure sign that it was not comfortably arranged in the first place, so try again. Sit in each chair and check for yourself. Is there a nearby light for reading, a smoker's stand or table for ash trays? Can you talk comfortably with your neighbor? Does the couch face the window so the light is in your eyes? A test like this will help in placing the furniture comfortably for all users.

The living room of the suite should be really colorful, gay, and interesting as a background for entertaining. Just remember to get sturdy furniture for use here, since large men and women, destructive children, and "wild" parties take a heavy toll of a room too daintily furnished. Suitability for purpose or, in one word, "functionalism," should be our motto. Keep up-to-date on arrangements. It is very important.

Wall Decorations

We mentioned at the start that decoration should be suitable to the place, so if you have a chance to play up the local scenery, do so.

Is there an artist in your town? His paintings or the color photographs taken and enlarged by a local man can be a good bit of local public relations and, if exhibited before hanging in the rooms, will be excellent publicity.

If your house over looks mountains or ocean, perhaps venetian blinds without curtains and with plain drapes will show guests your thoughtfulness. Be sure to tell them about it, somewhat as follows: "We are sure the view is one reason you have come to us and to help you enjoy it, we have omitted glass curtains. If you prefer them, just let us know." In one place, only one guest asked for the glass curtains. So they save laundry cost and the expense of buying the curtains for every window in the house.

The importance of really beautiful pictures is so well known that we seldom see the tiny or poor ones which were so prevalent. If you have small ones of good color and artistic value, do use them in groups, but only one such treatment to a room.

Usually only one or, at most, two walls need pictures, especially if there are windows on two or more sides of the room as draperies give interest there.

Today's guests in hotels and motels are not satisfied to find them "homelike." They expect to get the latest decorative ideas to take back with them for their own use and to impress the neighbors. Because of this, and also because of the fact that many experts are specializing in redecorating "Hospitality Centers" of all kinds are now more maintenance conscious. Decorators are often engaged for any sizeable project. The wise housekeeper welcomes relief from this duty and learns all she can by co-operating closely in the many things which remain under her supervision. You may sometimes be able to aid in saving money by asking questions, but never try to make suggestions, as most decorators are not accustomed to accepting them from people outside the profession.

Does your locality have some special historical significance? That is often a decorative asset and "conversation piece" back home. In Providence, R. I., the story of Roger Williams was used as the china design at one time. "Johnny Appleseed" was made use of in one place, and many other colorful characters have inspired interesting decor. The varied delightful murals or less expensive scenic papers of the surrounding country sometimes have added a few day's stay of vacationers. Special distinguishing qualities which have brought fame or popularity to an establishment should be retained, but not in a static condition, for their appeal can be enhanced by new touches of color and modern arrangement. Avoid all that gives an "institutional" look.

When there is an outside decorator, the housekeeper should be given information as to sources of supply of all new things, so she can contact them for information as to any problems of caring for them. When guests ask where they can get similar things, the decorator's name and address should be given as the source of information.

CHAPTER **23**

Treatment of Floor Coverings, Walls and Windows

Floor Coverings

The floors in most institutions are usually of cement as a fire pre-
ventive measure, but the housekeeper is often consulted about the
selection of floor coverings for them, so must be familiar with the
qualities of those for use under differing conditions. An unwise
choice can be very expensive. Carpet gives an effect of elegance and
is appropriate for most suites, bedrooms, lobby, dining-room, or
cocktail lounge, when chosen with both beauty·and durability in
mind.

Carpets

Where carpet is used, it is usually the largest initial expense in
furnishing a room. Hence, it often governs the choice of the decorative style and color. It is purchased largely from samples. For a
sizeable purchase it can be made to order in special design and color.

The best known carpets are Chenille, Velvet, Wilton, and Axminster.

Chenille is usually expensive as it is often custom made. It has a
heavy woolen back so it is almost a complete animal fiber product.
It is very adaptable, can use any type of yarn, be of any width up to
30 feet, any shape, color, design, and any one of four depths of pile.
It is too costly for the ordinary hotel budget but it is used where
elegance rather than cost governs the selection.

Velvet is the simplest type of weave and the best grades are very
durable, closely woven, almost all pile on the surface, and often solid
color (although it can have a figured design) , nine wires to the inch
being the best quality. These wires are knife-edged to cut the pile as
it is drawn out, thus producing the velvety appearance. It can be

137

woven over regular wires and left uncut. This forms a loop pile which does not show foot prints as easily and is called "Tapestry."

Velvet carpet can be bought in 27″ width—sometimes called three-quarter width—and also in 9′, 12′, 15′ or 18′ (broadloom) and is excellent for large spaces as there are no seams to show wear.

Velvet is good for the luxury suites where a rich appearance is the aim, and where the tariff warrants fairly frequent redecoration.

Wilton is a high-grade carpet for general use. The short pile type of good quality is popular for hotels because it does not crush easily and can stand heavy traffic. It is usually figured. A well-covered pattern, not too large in design, is considered best for bedrooms as it does not show spots, stains, burns, or wear as easily as a plain carpet does.

Designs are clean cut as they are made on a Jacquard loom. All colored yarns (except one that is brought to the surface to form the pattern) are woven in the body of the rug, acting as a cushion and adding to the luxurious feeling. From three to six different colored yarns may be used, but the best budget value is two colors. Good quality Wiltons contain little sizing and seldom have jute backing so they are good for damp climates.

Wilton is especially popular where a striking design is wanted as in a lobby and dining room. It is also good where structural defects make it advisable to paint all the walls the same color. In this case it can serve as the foundation for a bedroom's color scheme, with walls, draperies, upholstery, and spreads chosen to blend with its colors and design. Wilton is the best buy for stairs, corridors, and public rooms—any area subjected to heavy traffic.

Axminster has a higher pile than Wilton or velvet although usually fewer tufts to the square inch. This allows dirt, sand, and grit to go through and wear out the nap at the base of the pile, unless vacuumed very often. The better grades wear well if kept clean. A good rug cushion is necessary.

It is usually not as expensive as Wilton, and the colors and design are equally good, so it is acceptable to the decorator. Axminster is often used in guest rooms and is generally satisfactory if of good quality.

All nylon carpet is another expensive type. This restricts its use although it is said to be more durable than all wool. It has many admirable qualities. The decorator likes its clear colors. The housekeeper enjoys the ease with which it can be spot-cleaned. Because nylon fiber is smooth, not notched like wool, it is more soil resistant. Coffee, grease, and even protein stains are easily removed by soap and water, carbon tetrachloride or benzene. It is moth resistant and dries quickly after shampooing because it absorbs only one-third as much water as does wool, which it equals in color fastness.

It is tough, though pliable, and wears extremely well. The Dupont Golf Club lounge in Wilmington has a carpet that has been down for about seven years and it is claimed that spiked shoes have little effect on it. The chief fault with all-nylon carpet, I am told, is that a burn melts the fiber so that it cannot be mended like wool, but must have a piece set in. It has a static resistance to a vacuum, which is less than it was, and the company is working on a treatment which will remove this handicap.

The addition of nylon and rayon to wool in carpet in the right proportion is claimed to increase the durability. These blends, along with those of other synthetic fibers, are increasing in use because wool imports are fewer than formerly. Carpet wool has been largely imported from the mountain regions of Tibet, India, Scotland, South America, Iceland, and other countries where the climate is cold and the country rugged. Sheep under these conditions grow wool that is tough and firm and with plenty of resiliency.

Wall-to-wall carpet is at present high style, and increases the apparent size of the room. The room-size rug can be turned often however so it will wear evenly.

Hotels in tropical climates which close part of the year usually avoid moths, carpet beetles, and mildew trouble by using room-size rugs instead of wall-to-wall carpets, so they can be taken up, cleaned and properly stored while the house is closed. Rugs also have the advantage of being reversible so they will wear longer.

Cotton and linen rugs or a mixture of the two are being widely advertised. They have been found to be most satisfactory where they are no larger than can be put through the washer.

To be sure that you have considered all the necessary points it is advisable:

1. Deal only with reliable concerns.
2. Get several manufacturer's representatives to submit samples of the type, grade, design, and color they consider best for the special place it is to go, and for the type and location of the house.
3. Buy the best quality your budget will allow. All of the manufacturers offer valuable advice on choosing carpets and are only too glad to put their decorative staff at work on any of your problems involving color or design if the order is large enough. This is one reason for buying the same kind for several rooms.

Other Floor Coverings

Hospitals, dormitories and other large institutions have been quantity users of many other kinds of floor coverings for years. It is only recently that increased beauty of design plus extra durability and ease of maintenance have recommended them to hotels and clubs. Carpet wear and soil have been such a headache in public rooms that many of the smaller places are changing to various other types of flooring—rubber, cork, asphalt, vinyl tile, or linoleum floors. All are more durable than carpet if properly laid and if the right cleaning process is used. These are well suited for use in dining rooms where only small patches of the floor can be seen and in other places where traffic lanes are a problem. Here again, color and design may be a personal matter and the manufacturers aim to please.

Many of the older hotels have marble floors in the lobby, marble stairs, and borders to corridor rugs. This condition allows for a cooling effect in summer by the removal of the heavy winter rugs and is also an economy measure as the carpets are thus given at least three months' less wear annually. Smaller summer rugs may be used if the marble floor is too badly stained or worn.

Terrazzo floors in the past were usually a dull gray or tan but now brighter colors are introduced with pleasing decorative effect in lobbies, coffee shops, cocktail rooms, hallways, and in lavatories.

Some institutions have hardwood floors in many public rooms. These can be a beautiful and important part of the decor, when properly maintained.

WALL TREATMENTS

Walls can be treated in so many ways, with suc. ·greeable results. The only thing needed is a definite decision as to the effect desired. Paint and paper can be used to make rooms look larger or smaller, ceilings higher or lower, to disguise architectural errors, to give an effect of warmth or coolness, quietness or "busyness," formality or gaiety.

Painted Walls

It must be remembered that walls are the background for furnishings. If painted walls are chosen, light, modern furniture can be used against rather brilliant rich hues with satisfactory results—turquoise, luggage tan, a certain dusty rose, or a copper beige. The darker traditional furniture usually shows to advantage against the softer greyed tones that will fit into the color scheme.

Painted walls have the advantage of allowing more colorful designs in textures and carpets. They are easy to clean and often less expensive than papered walls. The newer paints are more easily washed and last longer.

Papered Walls

The papered wall adds interest and design where carpet, upholstery, and draperies are plain or striped. Paper may be used to good effect for a bed alcove or on one wall only. Today there are finishes for wall paper that make it very durable and cleanable and it is not always too expensive for the budget. One other thing to be considered in the room for the transient occupant is to keep it quiet in tone if it is no a busy, noisy street.

Public Rooms

Remember that these places are seen by local people and visitors who do not use the sleeping quarters. Therefore, they should be very colorful and dramatic to impress the public with the fact that the house is very fine and up-to-the-minute. Be particularly careful in dining rooms or cocktail lounges for certain colors make people look wan and food unappetizing.

No one should attempt to decorate a public room who has not already had some success with the ordinary bedroom and also a suite, during which she has learned how to use color and design to achieve certain effects.

It is always wise to place a large sample of paint or paper on the wall before deciding on its use and to see the result under the regular night lighting of the room, as well as daylight. Many times the effect is entirely different and not always equally pleasing. Naturally the choice should be governed by the customary light when the room is in use. The cocktail lounge is probably used most under artificial light while the coffee shop has daylight for the majority of the time it is open.

Here again the housekeeper can get valuable aid from all the best paint and paper companies who are anxious that their products shall be used to the best advantage.

Windows

Window treatment will depend largely on the size of both room and windows, the use of the room, and whether the floor covering is plain or figured.

In the ballroom, where the windows are often tall as well as wide and where the dance floor is plain, there can be a very dramatic use of large-scale design of strong color on a satin, or heavy silk background or on plain velvet to get the desired effect of elegance.

In a dining room, the same type of windows might have a very different treatment because of the carpet design. It could still be dramatic but perhaps not quite so elegant and with a gayer note.

The lobby also would differ according to the lighting. In one lobby I saw a colorful, really satisfactory effect created by the use of a very glossy plain turquoise satin for winter when the rugs were down, and a large-scale design on a wedgewood blue glossy satin background for summer when the marble floors were exposed. Later a change to a gold-flecked textured material was not nearly so effective because of the peculiar lighting.

In the suite where a feeling of gaiety is wanted, the window hangings can be of amusing design, but will naturally be simpler and more tailored in style. Venetian blinds are often used so no glass curtains are needed. The original idea in buying venetian blinds was to avoid constant laundry expense and to keep up with the times.

The faults of the old types of wooden or metal blinds which rattled so one could not sleep or did not close tightly enough to keep the sun out have been so improved that their use is still extensive. However, they do add a few minutes of dusting in every room the maid services and also for the vacuum man on cleaning days.

Where glass curtains are used, there is wide difference of opinion as to the comparative durability and cost of upkeep for those made of cotton, glass, nylon, orlon, and dacron. Curtain materials are apt to be chosen according to the type of laundry work done and the past experience of the housekeeper with any particular fabric or the choice of the manager or decorator may be the deciding factor.

CHAPTER 24

Upholstery and Drapery Fabrics and Accessories

There are now very satisfactory treatments to make all decorative fabrics more durable without reducing their luster and other attractive qualities. Materials of man-made fibers or their combination with natural ones are being made dust repellent, easy to clean, sun and tub fast, fire and water proof. Manufacturers are doing everything possible to lower institutional maintenance cost without reducing the beauty of color, design, or finish.

The use of metallic or gleaming synthetic threads in designs of drapery and upholstery materials make them much more interesting, where suitable.

Naturally, the style of furniture, modern, traditional, or period should be a factor in deciding on design for upholstery, and there are beautiful, not too expensive, fabrics to meet these different needs.

The proportions of a room and the scale of furniture also share in determining size and type of design for these fabrics. In small rooms, small but distinctive and somewhat less brilliant colors are used than in larger places.

Upholstery materials are more interesting than ever these days in texture, in the use of metallic or synthetic fibers as well as color and design. This is especially helpful in small rooms where one must be so careful not to use large patterns, yet get an effect that will appeal to patrons. Guests are looking for ideas to try out in their homes where rooms are not too large.

All of the best concerns selling decorative materials are only too glad to submit samples, offer suggestions as to color schemes, and help the housekeeper in every way possible.

Accessories

Those items which are not included under actual furnishings, but which add to the interest and satisfying decor of a room, we call accessories. Perhaps lamps might properly be considered furnishings because they are really necessary. However, the fact that, in addition to their primary function, they are supposed to add beauty of form, design and color, classes them in this category. We must never forget that there can be as much or more beauty in the lamp of simple design that is easier to keep clean.

Pictures, when not used as a starting point for the color scheme, are definitely selected to add color and interest to the walls and most people agree that they seem necessary on the plain painted wall. "Not too many" is the usual rule for hotel rooms. Perhaps there should be one large picture over the couch or fireplace and one, or at most two, groupings of smaller ones, similar in character, usually identically framed, in the parlor of a suite. Usually we find one large one over desk or bed in the sleeping room. Often there is a dresser with mirror opposite the bed which reflects the picture for the one lying there. Naturally those in the bedroom should be softer in tone and quieter in effect than the gaily colored, striking compositions in the room used for gay gatherings.

When undecided about the addition of another picture, it is sometimes wise to use a mirror instead. The size, shape and type, whether etched or plain, framed or not, depends on the style of furnishings as well as the taste of the decorator.

In some living rooms, a beautiful clock takes the place of a picture. You have all seen the toile or sunburst or banjo type which was most effective in the right setting.

Bright-hued pillows for the couch can add zest to a room, while over-sized colorful ash trays and vases ready to hold the flowers that so often are sent to hotel guests are good accents. Plants, when feasible, are a delightful home-like touch.

CHAPTER 25

The Executive Housekeeper

We have seen the variety and importance of some of the executive housekeeper's responsibilities, so now let us see what sort of person is needed to fill the position successfully. Here are a few qualifications she must have.

1. Excellent health, to survive the hectic days of demanding duties, with never any two days alike. No one who likes to go along smoothly in a rut could last long. Only a person who dislikes monotony and who is in excellent physical condition has the vitality, calm nerves, untiring energy and a real zest for this kind of work, can take it.

2. Her manner, appearance and personality must be such as to merit the respect and confidence of her staff. She needs to be well balanced, good natured, emotionally adult; optimistic but realistic; tactful and patient; fair and just; with an understanding of and love for all kinds of people. Naturally there is need for the qualities of leadership, integrity, tact, the invigorating force of inspiration and the ability to give clear, definite instructions. A real interest in her employees is important.

3. A real executive will organize her work so as to delegate to her assistants all possible responsibility for details so that her time can be spent on matters beyond their capability. Job analysis and specification are even more necessary for supervisors than for those they direct, so that is one of the department head's important duties. There are many other kinds of ability helpful to a person in this work. In fact, the more varied her education and experience, the better qualified she is for unexpected occurrences. All she knows will be of use at some time in this position.

4. The manager expects a dependable level-headed person, able to meet emergencies adequately, to keep a strict supervision over costs, train her employees to be not only efficient workers but pleasant, courteous people whose services are satisfactory to guests. He looks for close co-operation with all other department heads and depends on her for translating company policies and directives to employees and informing him of their reactions. He does not want her to bother him with petty matters but when a problem needs his attention and decision, he appreciates it if she tells how she has thought of solving it and asks his opinion. He may not agree with the idea but is glad the problem was not just thrown in his lap.

5. Today's department heads are all expected to be a part of the "management team," which considers with top management the many problems of the organization as a whole. It is necessary, therefore, for these executives to understand the policies of the institution in order to think constructively about matters outside their own sphere of action. They must realize that it is necessary to see their function in relation to the whole operation and be willing to wait for some justifiable expenditures because of a vital need elsewhere. Where this attitude prevails, there is greater co-ordination, more harmony, and smoother functioning of the entire organization. To be an effective member of this group, however, one must be able to look at the problem under consideration impersonally, not an easy thing to do, possible only when this attitude is habitual—in dealing with employees, for instance.

Education and Experience

So often the question is asked "How does one get into this work? What education is needed?" Until 1930, it was a top job, toward which the ambitious worked and finally reached. Dealing with situations as they came up were largely by trial and error, and often not effective. Until that date very few housekeepers of large institutions knew each other, so there was little exchange of ideas. Largely through the efforts of the Ahrens Publishing Company's editorial team the National Executive Housekeepers Association was formed in 1930.

The aims of the National Executive Housekeepers Association were to improve methods of work; enable the members to discuss their problems and so learn how others solved them; to have hotel managers and hospital administrators tell at their meetings what was expected of their housekeepers and, most important, to encourage education along the lines needed for the position in an attempt to give this position professional standing. These are only a few of the aims of this organization but the years since its formation have proved the worth of all of them. During this time, many increasingly important duties have been added to this Executive and the educational project has been of great value, so much so that various colleges have now a four year course, leading to a B.S. degree in housekeeping, after a year of internship. This is of great assistance to the young folks choosing this occupation for their life work but the N.E.H.A. is also assisting those now on the job by many courses, seminars, workshops, and lectures to increase their value to the institutions they serve. These are largely sponsored by Chapters in all parts of the country.

Many of those executive housekeepers are business women from a wide variety of industries, who find this work both challenging and rewarding. We would say then that fundamental academic instruction, followed by experience acquired under skilled supervision is the best way of training for this truly executive position with professional standing.

Following are the "core" subjects offered in the colleges mentioned.

Basic Social Sciences—Sociology, Psychology, Economics.

1. Orientation and Introduction to Institutional Housekeeping.
2. Personnel Management
   Human, Employee, Labor and Professional Relations.
   Wage Determination, Handling Interviews, Motivation, Allocation, and Communications.
3. Purchasing
   Evaluation of Source Information, Market Organization.
   Basic Interior Design.
   Textiles.
   Choice of Equipment and Cleaning Products.

Records.

Budgeting

4. Maintenance and Controls.

Safety.

Sanitation.

5. The necessary English. Chemistry, Physics and other topics as determined by the various colleges.

The value of research and an open mind toward new products is valuable but the housekeeper must be able to evaluate the inventions with regard to the budget as well as the usefulness in her work.

For those now employed in this capacity, who realize the need for supplementing their practical experience with educational courses, there are the Cornell Refresher Course in Hotel Housekeeping, the Michigan State University Course for Hospital Housekeepers and many other ways of keeping up to date on new products, methods of work, decorative know-how and so many other worthwhile subjects. Do not forget the housekeeper *cannot* stop learning if she wants to retain her standing as an executive. She *must* change with the times or be left behind.

Glossary

A.H.	Airline holdover
B	Baggage packed ready for departure or change to another room
Check-In	New arrival in room
Check-Out	Departure from the room
Closet Count	Amount of linen in maid's closet
Comp.	No charge for room
Contract Work	Work done by outside concerns
D.R.	Room occupied for day only; day rate
Discards	Linen or other articles too badly worn, torn, stained, or burned to be used for guests
Drop Cloths	Heavy cloths used by workmen to protect furniture and carpets
Floats	A term used in describing table linen. Floats are the warp threads which pass over more than one weft thread to form a pattern
G.	Guarantee that room will be paid for even if not used
Grommets	Metal rings inserted in the upper hem of shower curtains to reinforce the material so it may be hung on bar hooks without danger of tearing
HC	House Count—the number of guests accommodated over night
I.O.	In order—room ready for occupancy
L.B.	Light baggage—only a few personal belongings or a small bag in the room

L.O.	Lockout; the guest cannot get into the room until he speaks with the manager
M	Make-up. A room left by the day maid for the night maid to handle; it may be either a check-out or an occupied room
N.B.	No baggage; possibly a day occupancy or a prepaid account
N.R.	No reservation
OC	Occupied with baggage
OOO	Out of order for cleaning, repairs, or renovation
P	Permanent guest
PP	Prepaid
Pass Sticker	Any package taken out of the building by an employee must have a sticker with the signature of the department head on it. It must be sealed so it cannot be opened without detection between the time it leaves the office and is given to the timekeeper
R.C.	Room count—number of rooms occupied over night
S.O.	Sleep-out. Room not occupied but baggage still in the room
Section	Rooms assigned to one maid for servicing
Shortage	Amount of linen less than last count including discards and known losses
Spot Check	A check on the condition of one or more rooms in each section
Telautograph	An instrument which may be written on by hand and which carries the message from one department to others
Three-Par Stock	Three times the number of pieces of linen needed to make up all the rooms in the house
V	Vacant room

VIP	Very important person requiring special attention
Vacancy List	A record which the maid makes each morning of the rooms in her section—whether occupied, check-out, sleep-out, etc.
W.L.	On waiting list
Warp	Threads running lengthwise in linens
Weft or Woof	Threads running crosswise in linens

Index

155